BAKING
Vegan
Bread
AT HOME

Baking Vegan Bread at Home

Beautiful Everyday and Artisan Plant-Based Breads

Shane Martin

HARVARD
COMMON
PRESS

Quarto.com

© 2024 Quarto Publishing Group USA Inc.
Text © 2024 Shane Martin

First Published in 2024 by The Harvard Common Press, an imprint of The Quarto Group,
100 Cummings Center, Suite 265-D, Beverly, MA 01915, USA.
T (978) 282-9590 F (978) 283-2742

The Harvard Common Press titles are also available at discount for retail, wholesale, promotional, and bulk purchase. For details, contact the Special Sales Manager by email at specialsales@quarto.com or by mail at The Quarto Group, Attn: Special Sales Manager, 100 Cummings Center, Suite 265-D, Beverly, MA 01915, USA.

28 27 26 25 24   1 2 3 4 5

ISBN: 978-0-7603-8624-8

Digital edition published in 2024
eISBN: 978-0-7603-8625-5

Library of Congress Cataloging-in-Publication Data is available.

Design and Page Layout: Tanya Jacobson, tanyajacobson.co
Photography: Shane Martin
Illustration: Shutterstock

Printed in China

To Rusty and Becky,

In loving memory of my mom and dad, two extraordinary souls who touched my life and every life around them with their warmth, kindness, and protection.

Although you never had the chance to see me achieve my dream of being a food blogger or writing a book, your love and guidance continue to inspire me every day. This book is dedicated to both of you, my greatest cheerleaders, who continue to inspire me to chase my dreams and share my love for food and storytelling with the world. Your love and legacy will forever be the driving force behind my journey as a food blogger and writer.

With all my love,

Your son, Shane

CONTENTS

INTRODUCTION

The Pleasures and Craft of Vegan Bread Baking

Welcome to the aromatic world of vegan bread baking! In this cookbook, we are going to embark on a journey to discover the wonders of plant-based bread, where creativity, health, and compassion intertwine. Whether you're a seasoned vegan or a curious food enthusiast looking to explore new horizons, whether you're a pro baker or a beginner with flour-covered hands, this collection of recipes and tips will equip you with the knowledge and skills to master the art of vegan breadmaking.

Vegan bread? For some home cooks, the thought of baking without the holy trinity of eggs, milk, and butter seems sacrilegious. But trust me—with the right ingredients and techniques, vegan bread is just as satisfying as, if not better than, its dairy- and egg-laden counterparts. Yes, I am placing in your hands the power to make bread so tasty it's guaranteed to make all the dairy devotees drool and beg for more. Pretty cool, huh?

So how did I come to write this book? I'm very passionate about cooking. I went vegan more than ten years ago primarily for health reasons and, not to sound too dramatic, it literally saved my life. I set out on a mission not so much to *make vegan food* but to *make food vegan*: I wanted to find ways to put a plant-based spin on some of my favorite recipes, breads included. There has been a lot of trial and error over these ten years. It was like learning to cook all over again—though to say it was worth it would be an understatement. And I have learned, through all of that experimentation, a decent amount about the art and science of baking vegan breads. I'm just a normal, hard-working dude—well, admittedly one who writes a vegan food blog for home cooks—and I am thrilled to share what I know with you in these pages.

Hopefully you agree with me (if not now, after the first bite of your homemade bread): Bread is awesome. I take the position of the many great religious leaders throughout history who have referred to bread as "life." I love bread! And, if loving bread is wrong, I don't want to be right. That being said, this cookbook is not just about bread; it's also about empowering you, dear reader, to experiment and personalize your breadmaking adventures. Don't shy away from trying out new flavor combinations or incorporating unique ingredients. Let your creative baker's soul soar like a fluffy sourdough starter! Embrace the learning process and don't be disheartened if your first few attempts don't turn out exactly as you envisioned. The journey to becoming a master vegan bread baker is filled with twists and turns, but the end result is oh-so-rewarding. So let's roll up our sleeves, flour our noses, and get ready to create magic with our vegan bread.

THE VEGAN BAKER'S PANTRY ESSENTIALS

Before we embark on our breadmaking adventure, let's take a peek inside the vegan baker's pantry. You might be surprised at how many of these items you already have; nevertheless, it's important to keep your shelves stocked with an array of plant-powered ingredients so you'll be ready at a moment's notice to bring your bread recipes to life.

Flour Power

It all starts with good flour, and I don't like to skimp on this ingredient. You wouldn't want to breathe bad air, would you? Exactly—don't use crappy flour. Stock the pantry with organic unbleached flour, whole wheat flour, spelt flour, bread flour, and good gluten-free flour specifically for baking bread. Almond flour, despite its popularity among health-conscious cooks, *will not work* for the vast majority of vegan breads.

Yeast

I use active dry yeast and instant dry yeast in my bread recipes. Active dry yeast describes any yeast that needs to be activated with warm liquid before it's used, while instant dry yeast is one that's ready the moment you open the packet. Instant dry yeast is often called rapid or quick rise yeast; it does rise faster than active dry yeast. A packet of yeast is 2¼ teaspoons (7 g).

OAT FLOUR
DARK RYE
GLUTEN FREE
WHOLE WHEAT

Sweeteners

Cane sugar, maple syrup, and agave are great sweeteners to replace regular table sugar, which is not always vegan.

Binders and Egg Replacers

Ground flaxseed or flaxseed meal, chia seeds, and unsweetened applesauce are good options. In this book, we'll also be using something called a flax "egg": 1 tablespoon (7 g) ground flaxseed mixed with 3 tablespoons (45 ml) water. Another interesting ingredient is aquafaba; this is the liquid drained from a can of chickpeas. It can stand in for egg whites.

Plant-Based Milks

Almond milk, soy milk, oat milk, coconut milk, and cashew milk are all great options. Always use the unsweetened version. I call for specific milk in some recipes, but you can always substitute your preferred type.

Fats

Vegan butter, vegetable oil, avocado oil, and coconut oil are good fats for baking bread. This is another ingredient that you can usually choose your preferred type—just pay attention to whether the fat has to be liquid or solid.

Leavening Agents

Baking powder and baking soda are important when it comes to baking. They cause the dough to expand by releasing gas once mixed with liquid, acid, or heat. Leavening agents also give baked goods optimal volume, texture, and crumb.

Vinegar

Apple cider vinegar adds a tangy flavor and also activates baking soda.

Spices and Herbs

It's great to always keep your spice rack stacked because this is where you can get creative and add so much depth of flavor to a bread. Common spices that work great in breads are cinnamon, nutmeg, rosemary, garlic powder, onion powder, and thyme.

Nuts and Seeds

Almonds, walnuts, sunflower seeds, and pumpkin seeds are great for adding healthy fats, texture, and bulk to hearty whole-grain breads.

ACTIVATING THE YEAST

In many recipes, I'll say you should have warm water to activate the yeast. The water should be around 110°F (43°C). It is important that the water isn't too hot, or it will kill the yeast. An easy way to make water the right temperature is to combine 2 parts cold water with 1 part boiling water. I recommend using a kitchen thermometer for this. If the water is too hot, it will kill the yeast. If not warm enough, it won't activate the yeast. Another way is to measure room-temperature water in a mug and microwave on high for 20 to 25 seconds.

TOOLS OF THE TRADE

When baking vegan bread, having the right tools can make the process smoother and more enjoyable. While having these tools can enhance your baking experience, not all of them are needed to make every recipe in this book. So don't worry if you're missing a few items. Just improvise with what you have and enjoy the process of baking delicious vegan bread!

Mixing Bowls

Have a variety of mixing bowls in different sizes. This allows you to mix different ingredients separately and efficiently.

Measuring Cups and Spoons

Accurate measurements are crucial in baking. Invest in a set of measuring cups and spoons to ensure your ingredients are measured precisely.

Stand Mixer or Hand Mixer

While not essential, a stand mixer or hand mixer can save you time and effort when kneading dough or mixing ingredients. It's especially helpful for recipes that require more prolonged mixing. A stand mixer equipped with a dough hook is especially useful.

Dough Scraper

A dough scraper is handy for easily scraping dough from bowls or countertops, as well as for dividing or shaping the dough.

Bread Pans or Loaf Tins

Depending on the type of bread you're baking, having good-quality bread pans or loaf tins is essential. Opt for nonstick pans or line them with parchment paper to prevent sticking. A standard loaf pan is 8½ x 4½ x 2½ inches (21 x 11 x 6 cm), but you can use any size you have on hand—just be sure to adjust the recipe yield.

INTRODUCTION 13

Baking Stone or Pizza Stone

A baking stone or pizza stone is beneficial for achieving a crisp crust. Preheat the stone in the oven, then place the bread on top to bake.

Bread Lame

A bread lame (meaning "blade" in French and pronounced "lahm") is a tool specifically designed for scoring dough. You can also use a sharp serrated knife to create cuts or designs on the surface of the bread. This allows the dough to expand properly while baking.

Oven Thermometer

Ensure that your oven is accurately heated by using an oven thermometer. This helps to maintain the correct baking temperature and ensures consistent results.

Kitchen Timer

A kitchen timer or a timer app on your cell phone helps you keep track of baking and proofing times. This ensures your bread is baked to perfection without over- or undercooking.

Cooling Mat or Wire Rack

Place your baked bread on a cooling mat or wire rack to prevent condensation from building up, which will make the bottom of the loaf soggy.

Bread Box or Other Bread Storage Container

Once your bread has cooled, store it in a bread storage container, such as a bread box, or wrap it in a clean tea towel to maintain its freshness.

Parchment Paper

This is great for lining baking sheets or loaf pans and eliminates the need for greasing your pans. It also makes cleanup a breeze.

Plastic Wrap

When proofing your dough and letting it rise, it always needs to be covered; plastic wrap is perfect.

GLUTEN-FREE OPTIONS

For those with gluten sensitivities or celiac disease, there'll be a few options in this book for you as we go along. Together we'll explore a range of gluten-free flours and discuss tips and tricks to ensure your gluten-free vegan bread is moist, flavorful, and oh-so-satisfying.

BAKING BRILLIANCE: TIPS AND TECHNIQUES

When baking vegan bread, there are several important tips to keep in mind to ensure successful results. We'll delve into specifics within the recipes, but here are some key issues to keep in mind.

Knead to Know

Kneading is where the magic happens in breadmaking. From traditional hand kneading to the modern stand mixer, the goal is to achieve that perfect elastic dough every time—and it depends on a variety of factors. Together, we'll take everything into account as we approach each recipe.

Secrets to a Crisp Crust and Tender Crumb

The holy grail of bread baking: Achieving that elusive balance between a crispy crust and a tender crumb. And, yes, it's totally possible to do with vegan bread. The perfect texture in your vegan bread will leave your taste buds singing with delight. This is another factor that we'll explore in more detail in the recipes.

Understand Your Ingredients

Familiarize yourself with vegan substitutes for common baking ingredients such as eggs, dairy, and honey. This includes options like flaxseed meal or chia seeds mixed with water as an egg replacement, plant-based milk alternatives, and sweeteners like maple syrup or agave nectar.

Choose the Right Flour

Experiment with different types of flours to find the one that suits your recipe best. Whole wheat flour, spelt flour, and bread flour are popular choices for vegan bread. Flip through the recipes to see what is used where to get a feel for selection.

Pay Attention to Hydration

Vegan bread doughs can require slightly more liquid compared to traditional bread recipes. This is because some vegan ingredients, such as flaxseed meal, absorb moisture. You will need to adjust the liquid content gradually to achieve the desired dough consistency, ensuring it is not too dry or too sticky.

Incorporate Protein-Rich Ingredients

To enhance the texture and structure of your vegan bread, include protein-rich ingredients such as legume flours (e.g., chickpea flour) or add vital wheat gluten, especially when working with gluten-free flours (obviously, don't add vital wheat gluten if you have a gluten intolerance). These additions help to provide elasticity and structure to the dough.

Let the Bread Rise and Rest

Proper proofing is crucial for a well-risen and flavorful loaf. Give the yeast enough time to work its magic and allow the dough to rise until doubled in size. After shaping the dough, allow it to rest again before baking. This resting period helps the gluten relax and improves the texture of the final product.

Enhance Flavor with Spices and Fillings

Experiment with an array of spices, herbs, and fillings to add depth and complexity to your vegan bread. Cinnamon, nutmeg, garlic, rosemary, or even dried fruits and nuts can create delicious flavor combinations that will leave your taste buds delighted.

Maintain Proper Oven Temperature

Preheat your oven to the recommended temperature and use an oven thermometer to ensure accuracy. Proper temperature control is essential for even baking, achieving a golden crust, and avoiding under- or overbaking your bread.

Experiment and Have Fun

Vegan bread baking is an opportunity for creativity and exploration. First, if you want these recipes to turn out right, *follow the instructions*. Once you have a recipe down as written, don't be afraid to experiment with different flavors, shapes, and techniques. Enjoy the process and embrace the occasional mishaps; they often lead to unexpected discoveries and delicious results.

Remember, practice makes perfect, so don't get discouraged if your first attempt doesn't turn out exactly as planned. With these tips in mind and a playful spirit, you'll be well on your way to becoming a master of vegan bread baking.

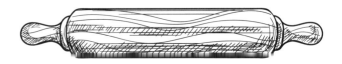

THE ESSENCE OF
BAKING VEGAN BREAD

My fellow bakers and aspiring vegan bread enthusiasts, we are embarking together on an epic journey through the realm of plant-based bread-making. We'll knead and rise together, and we'll certainly have our share of both baking blunders and delightful victories. Throughout this journey, I hope you will agree that this is a vegan bread cookbook that's a perfect balance of compassion, carb comas, and encouragement!

Baking vegan bread is not just about substituting ingredients, but rather about embracing a compassionate and sustainable lifestyle. Each loaf we craft holds the power to change the world, one bite at a time. Who would've thought that a simple act of mixing flour and water could have such a profound impact on our planet and its furry/feathered inhabitants?

If you're into the holistic natural realm, baking vegan bread is a marvelous way to connect with like-minded individuals who share our love for fluffy goodness and ethical living. So, my fellow bakers, let's create a community that supports and uplifts one another. Share your baking triumphs on social media, join baking clubs, or even host a vegan bread bake-off! There's nothing quite like bonding over perfectly proofed loaves and spreading kindness through the power of carbs.

Before I bid you adieu, I want to remind you that the essence of baking vegan bread goes far beyond the kitchen. It's about embracing a lifestyle of compassion, making conscious choices, and realizing that we all have the ability to make a positive impact on our environment and the beings we share it with. So, as you embark on your breadmaking escapades, remember to celebrate not just the end product but also the journey that got you there.

With a tinge of humor, a dash of encouragement, and a whole lot of love, let's continue baking our way to a better, kinder world, one loaf at a time. Happy baking, my friends, and may your loaves be forever fluffy and your hearts forever light!

See page 24 for Old-Style English Muffins recipe

CHAPTER 1

Muffins, Scones, and Other Breakfast Breads & Quick Breads

Old-Style English Muffins

English muffins are a breakfast staple loved by many around the world. These vegan English muffins are just as airy and delicious as their traditional counterparts. Serve them warm with your favorite vegan butter or jam, or create a scrumptious breakfast sandwich with tofu scramble, avocado, and fresh vegetables.

¼ cup (60 ml) water, warm (around 110°F [43°C])

1 tablespoon (13 g) organic cane sugar

1 packet or 2¼ teaspoons (7 g) instant yeast

2½ cups (313 g) organic unbleached all-purpose flour, plus more as needed

1 teaspoon (6 g) salt

1 cup (235 ml) unsweetened plant-based milk

2 tablespoons (30 ml) olive oil

Cornmeal for dusting

Makes 8 to 10 English muffins

1. In a small bowl, combine warm water and sugar. Sprinkle the instant yeast over the mixture and give it a gentle stir. Set it aside for about 5 to 10 minutes until the mixture becomes frothy.

2. In a large mixing bowl, combine the organic unbleached all-purpose flour and salt. Create a well in the center and pour in the activated yeast mixture, plant-based milk, and olive oil. Stir everything together with a wooden spoon or your hands until a shaggy dough forms.

3. Transfer the dough onto a lightly floured surface. Begin kneading the dough for about 5 to 7 minutes until it becomes smooth and elastic. If the dough feels too sticky, gradually add more flour, but be careful not to overdo it.

4. Shape the dough into a ball and place it in a lightly oiled bowl, turning it to coat all sides. Cover the bowl with a clean kitchen towel or plastic wrap and let it rise in a warm place for approximately 1 to 2 hours until it has doubled in size.

5. Preheat your oven to 375°F (190°C). Line a baking sheet with parchment paper and sprinkle it with cornmeal.

6. Once the dough has risen, punch it down to release any air bubbles. Transfer it to a floured surface and roll it out to a thickness of about ½ inch (1 cm). Use a round cookie cutter or a glass to cut out individual muffins. Place them on the prepared baking sheet, spacing them about 1 inch (2.5 cm) apart.

7. Cover the baking sheet with a clean kitchen towel or plastic wrap and let the muffins rise for an additional 30 to 45 minutes until they have puffed up slightly.

8. Heat a nonstick skillet over medium heat. Carefully transfer the muffins to the skillet, cooking them for about 1 minute on each side until they turn golden brown. You can cook them in batches, depending on the size of your skillet.

9. Once both sides are nicely browned, transfer the muffins back to the baking sheet and bake them in the preheated oven for about 10 to 12 minutes to ensure they are cooked through. Allow them to cool slightly before prying them open with a fork. (Poking around the center with a fork instead of slicing through with a knife reveals a nice irregular surface dotted with little bubbles.)

When Life Gives You Lemon Muffins

These muffins are the perfect combination of tangy and sweet, making them an irresistible treat for any time of the day. Bursting with zesty lemon flavor, these moist, fluffy, and entirely plant-based muffins are easy to make and require simple ingredients that you likely already have in your pantry. These delightful citrusy treats are sure to brighten up your day!

1½ cups (188 g) organic unbleached all-purpose flour

½ cup (100 g) organic cane sugar

2 teaspoons (9 g) baking powder

½ teaspoon (2 g) baking soda

¼ teaspoon (2 g) salt

1 cup (235 ml) unsweetened almond milk

⅓ cup (80 ml) vegetable oil

1 teaspoon (5 ml) vanilla extract

Zest of 2 lemons

Juice of 2 lemons, divided

1 tablespoon apple cider vinegar

1 cup (125 g) powdered sugar

Makes 12 muffins

1. Preheat your oven to 350°F (180°C). Line a muffin tin with paper liners or lightly grease them with oil.

2. Whisk together the flour, sugar, baking powder, baking soda, and salt until well combined.

3. In a separate bowl, combine the almond milk, oil, vanilla extract, lemon zest, juice of 1 lemon, and apple cider vinegar. Stir well to combine.

4. Pour the wet ingredients into the dry ingredients and gently mix until just combined. Be careful not to overmix, as this can result in dense muffins. Divide the batter equally among the prepared muffin cups, filling them about three-quarters full. Bake in the preheated oven for 18 to 20 minutes or until a toothpick inserted into the center of a muffin comes out clean.

5. While the muffins are baking, prepare the lemon glaze by whisking together the powdered sugar and juice of 1 lemon in a small bowl until smooth. Set aside.

6. Once the muffins are done, remove them from the oven and let them cool in the muffin tin for 5 minutes. Then transfer them to a wire rack to cool completely.

7. When the muffins are completely cooled, drizzle the lemon glaze over the top of each muffin. Allow the glaze to set for a few minutes before serving.

NOTE:
These muffins can be stored in an airtight container at room temperature for up to 3 days.

Everyday Blueberry Muffins

Bursting with juicy blueberries, these muffins are perfect for breakfast or as a delightful snack. The best part? They're sweet, fluffy, and reminiscent of all things good in the world—and that's even before slicing a warm muffin and slathering each half with melted vegan butter. Yum!

1 cup (235 ml) unsweetened oat milk

¾ cup (150 g) organic cane sugar

⅓ cup (80 ml) vegetable oil

1 teaspoon (5 ml) vanilla extract

2 cups (250 g) organic unbleached all-purpose flour

1 tablespoon (14 g) baking powder

¼ teaspoon (2 g) salt

1½ to 2 cups (225 to 300 g) fresh or frozen blueberries

Makes 12 muffins

1. Preheat oven to 350°F (180°C). Lightly spray a muffin tin with cooking spray or add paper cups.

2. Add the oat milk, sugar, oil, and vanilla to a small mixing bowl and whisk together until well combined.

3. In a large mixing bowl, combine the flour, baking powder, and salt.

4. Pour the wet mixture into the dry mixture and mix with a wooden spoon or spatula until just combined. Don't overmix, or you'll get very dense muffins. Gently fold the blueberries into the batter.

5. Fill each muffin hole with ¼ cup (60 ml) batter. Place in the oven and bake for 30 minutes. Let the muffins cool for a few minutes and enjoy.

STORING:

Counter and fridge: Once the muffins are cool, you can store them with a paper towel under and over them in a container on the counter for up to 3 days. You can store them in an airtight container in the refrigerator for up to a week.

Freezer: Once completely cooled, wrap the muffins individually and store them in a freezer-safe container for up to 2 months. When you're ready to eat them, let them thaw to room temperature.

Jalapeño Cheddar Cornbread Muffins

Muffins are a beloved treat, but they're not limited to only sweet flavors. If you're a fan of the combination of spicy jalapeños and the rich, tangy taste of cheddar, then you're in for a treat. These vegan muffins have a sweet, slightly spicy flavor, and are wonderfully cheesy thanks to the from-scratch cheese sauce. They pair perfectly with soup and chili.

For the cheddar cheese sauce:

1 cup (137 g) raw cashews (soaked for 10 minutes in hot water)

½ cup + 2 tablespoons (150 g) water

¼ cup (36 g) nutritional yeast

2 tablespoons (30 ml) lemon juice

½ teaspoon (3 g) salt

For the muffins:

1 cup (235 ml) unsweetened almond milk

1 tablespoon (15 ml) apple cider vinegar

1 cup (140 g) yellow cornmeal

1½ cups organic unbleached flour (188 g) or whole wheat pastry flour (144 g)

1 tablespoon (13.8 g) baking powder

½ teaspoon (3 g) salt

⅓ cup (80 ml) aquafaba

2 tablespoons (40 g) maple syrup

½ cup (65 g) frozen, fresh, or canned sweet corn

¼ cup (34 g) diced jalapeño pepper

Makes 12 muffins

To make the cheese sauce:

1. Drain the cashews after soaking and add to your blender with the water, nutritional yeast, lemon juice, and salt. Blend until smooth and creamy. Set aside.

To make the jalapeño cheddar cornbread muffins:

1. Preheat oven to 375°F (190°C) and line a muffin tin with paper liners or use a nonstick muffin pan.

2. Make vegan buttermilk by whisking together the almond milk and apple cider vinegar in a small bowl. Set aside and allow to curdle.

3. To a large mixing bowl, add the cornmeal, flour, baking powder, and salt and whisk together.

4. Add the vegan buttermilk, aquafaba, maple syrup, and cheddar cheese sauce to the dry ingredients. Stir until everything is just mixed. Don't overmix. Then, fold in the corn and diced jalapeños until well combined.

5. Spoon equal amounts of batter into the muffin pan cups. Place in the oven and bake for 22 minutes. Use a toothpick or small knife to check for doneness. Simply insert; if it comes out clean, the cornbread muffins are done. Let the muffins cool for a few minutes before removing and enjoying.

TIPS:

Leftovers can be kept for up to 5 days in an airtight container at room temperature or in the fridge.

These muffins freeze well. Wrap them individually and store for up to 3 months in the freezer.

Chocolate Chip Stone Scones

These delightful treats are a perfect fusion of buttery goodness and irresistible chocolatey indulgence, all while being completely plant-based. With a light and flaky texture, these scones are studded with rich and melty vegan chocolate chips that will satisfy any craving. It's time to indulge in the perfect blend of sweetness and decadence with every bite of these irresistible scones!

2 cups (250 g) organic unbleached all-purpose flour, plus more as needed

¼ cup (50 g) organic cane sugar

1 tablespoon (14 g) baking powder

½ teaspoon (3 g) salt

½ cup (112 g) vegan butter, chilled and cubed

¾ cup (175 ml) almond milk

1 teaspoon (5 ml) vanilla extract

½ cup (88 g) vegan chocolate chips

Makes 8 scones

1. Preheat your oven to 400°F (200°C) and line a baking sheet with parchment paper.

2. In a large mixing bowl, whisk together the flour, sugar, baking powder, and salt.

3. Add the chilled vegan butter to the dry ingredients. Use a pastry cutter or your fingertips to cut the butter into the flour mixture until it resembles coarse crumbs.

4. Make a well in the center of the mixture and pour in the almond milk and vanilla extract. Stir until just combined. Then, gently fold in the chocolate chips.

5. Transfer the dough onto a lightly floured surface. Knead it a few times until it comes together, being careful not to overwork it.

6. Shape the dough into a circle about 1 inch (2.5 cm) thick. Cut the circle into 8 equal wedges.

7. Place the scones onto the prepared baking sheet, leaving some space between them.

8. Bake for 15 to 18 minutes or until the scones are golden brown and cooked through.

9. Remove from the oven and let them cool slightly on a wire rack before serving.

Healthy Baked Chocolate Donuts

These delectable rings of chocolaty joy will leave you wondering how something so delicious could possibly be cruelty-free and vegan. Baked to perfection and coated with a rich chocolate glaze, these donuts are here to prove that veganism is no hole-y grail, but a delightfully indulgent journey to the dark (chocolate) side. So, grab your aprons, summon your inner baker, and get ready to bake up a storm of cocoa-infused bliss!

---

1 cup (125 g) organic unbleached all-purpose flour

¼ cup (22 g) unsweetened cocoa powder

½ cup (100 g) organic cane sugar

1 teaspoon (5 g) baking powder

½ teaspoon (2 g) baking soda

¼ teaspoon (2 g) salt

¾ cup (175 ml) almond milk

¼ cup (59 ml) vegetable oil, plus more as needed

1 teaspoon (5 ml) + ½ teaspoon (3 ml) vanilla extract, divided

½ cup (88 g) vegan chocolate chips

2 tablespoons (28 g) coconut oil

2 tablespoons (40 g) maple syrup

Optional toppings: Chopped nuts, shredded coconut, sprinkles

Makes 9 to 12 donuts

1. Preheat your oven to 350°F (180°C). Grease a donut pan with a little vegetable oil or use nonstick cooking spray.

2. In a large mixing bowl, whisk together the flour, cocoa powder, sugar, baking powder, baking soda, and salt until well combined.

3. Add almond milk, vegetable oil, and 1 teaspoon (5 ml) vanilla extract to the dry ingredients. Stir until the batter is smooth and there are no lumps.

4. Spoon the batter into a piping bag or a resealable plastic bag with a corner snipped off. Pipe the batter evenly into the greased donut pan, filling each cavity about three-quarters full.

5. Bake the donuts for 12 to 15 minutes or until a toothpick inserted into the donut comes out clean.

6. Remove the donuts from the oven and let them cool in the pan for a few minutes. Then transfer them to a wire rack to cool completely.

7. While the donuts are cooling, prepare the vegan chocolate glaze. In a microwave-safe bowl, combine the vegan chocolate chips and coconut oil. Microwave in 30-second intervals, stirring in between, until the chocolate chips are melted and smooth. Stir in the maple syrup and ½ teaspoon (3 ml) vanilla extract until well combined.

8. Dip each cooled donut into the chocolate glaze, letting the excess drip off, or use a spoon to spread the glaze over the donuts. Place the glazed donuts back on the wire rack to allow the glaze to set. Optional: Add your favorite toppings like chopped nuts, shredded coconut, or sprinkles while the glaze is still wet.

Beautiful Belgian Waffles

The fluffy texture and crispy exterior of Belgian waffles make them irresistible, whether for a weekend brunch or a special occasion. These mouthwatering waffles are just as delectable as their nonvegan counterparts, so break out the waffle bar toppings.

2 cups (250 g) organic unbleached all-purpose flour

2 tablespoons (26 g) organic cane sugar

1 tablespoon (13.8 g) baking powder

½ teaspoon (3 g) salt

2 cups (475 ml) unsweetened plant-based milk

⅓ cup (75 g) vegan butter, melted

1 teaspoon (5 ml) vanilla extract

Cooking spray for waffle iron

Makes 6 waffles

1. Preheat your Belgian waffle iron according to the manufacturer's instructions. In a large mixing bowl, whisk together the organic unbleached all-purpose flour, sugar, baking powder, and salt. Ensure that all the dry ingredients are well combined.

2. Create a well in the center of the dry mixture and pour in the plant-based milk, vegan butter, and vanilla extract. Stir until just combined. Be careful not to overmix; a few lumps are perfectly fine.

3. Allow the batter to rest for 5 to 10 minutes. This resting time allows the ingredients to hydrate and ensures a tender texture. Once the batter has rested, give it a gentle stir. If the batter seems too thick, you can add a splash of plant-based milk to achieve a pourable consistency.

4. Lightly grease the waffle iron with cooking spray. Pour an appropriate amount of batter onto the center of the iron, spreading it out gently to cover the surface. Close the lid and cook for the recommended time provided by your waffle iron's instructions until golden and crisp, usually 3 to 5 minutes.

5. Carefully remove the waffle from the iron using a fork or tongs. Place it on a wire rack to cool slightly, which helps to maintain its crispiness. Repeat the process with the remaining batter.

SERVING SUGGESTIONS:

Classic: Top your waffles with a generous drizzle of pure maple syrup and a sprinkle of powdered sugar. Add a few fresh berries or sliced bananas for an extra burst of flavor and color.

Indulgent: Amp up the decadence by adding a dollop of vegan whipped cream or a scoop of dairy-free ice cream. Finish it off with a drizzle of vegan chocolate sauce or caramel for an utterly irresistible treat.

Savory Twist: Belgian waffles aren't just for sweet toppings. Get creative and try savory combinations like avocado slices, sautéed mushrooms, vegan cheese, or vegan hollandaise sauce for a unique and delicious twist.

Oil-Free Fluffy Pancakes

When it comes to pancakes, there's something undeniably comforting about a tall stack of fluffy goodness drizzled with syrup. Made with just seven simple ingredients, they're completely plant-based and melt-in-your-mouth delicious. Saturday mornings never tasted so good.

1 cup (125 g) organic unbleached all-purpose flour

2 tablespoons (26 g) organic cane sugar

1 tablespoon (14 g) baking powder

¼ teaspoon (2 g) salt

1 cup (235 ml) unsweetened almond milk

1 tablespoon (15 ml) apple cider vinegar

1 teaspoon (5 ml) vanilla extract

Makes 4 large or 8 small pancakes

1. Add the flour, sugar, baking powder, and salt to a large mixing bowl and whisk to combine.

2. In a separate bowl, add the almond milk, vinegar, and vanilla and whisk until everything is well combined.

3. Form a well in the center of the dry mix, pour in the wet mixture, and stir with a wooden spoon or spatula until the batter is smooth but still has a few lumps. Don't overmix the pancakes or they'll be denser and won't rise as much. Set the batter aside and let it sit for 5 to 10 minutes.

4. Heat a nonstick skillet over medium heat; let the skillet heat completely before starting your first pancake. Pour ¼ cup (60 ml) batter on the surface. When the top of the pancake starts to bubble, flip with a spatula and cook for another 30 to 45 seconds. The edges should become slightly brown. Repeat with remaining batter. Move the cooked pancakes onto a covered plate as each finishes. Serve with warm maple syrup, fruit, or any of your favorite toppings.

Apple Banana Oat Muffins

These fruity, perfectly moist muffins are healthy and delicious, and so easy to make using only simple wholesome ingredients. Great as a quick-grab snack or breakfast! They are free of gluten, oil, and refined sugar.

3 cups (240 g) rolled oats (gluten-free)

2 teaspoons (9.2 g) baking powder

1 teaspoon (2 g) ground cinnamon

¼ teaspoon (1.5 g) salt

2 medium-sized apples or 1 cup (245 g) unsweetened applesauce

5 overripe bananas

¼ cup (80 g) maple syrup

3 tablespoons (45 ml) lemon juice

1 teaspoon (5 ml) vanilla extract

¾ cup (175 ml) water

Makes 6 large muffins or 12 regular muffins

1. Preheat the oven to 400°F (200°C). Line a large 6-cup muffin pan or a regular 12-cup cupcake pan with muffin liners or parchment paper. You could also use a silicone muffin pan.

2. Place the oats in a food processor or blender and blend until a coarse flour is formed. It should not be fine like regular flour but should have some texture. To a large mixing bowl, add the blended oats, baking powder, cinnamon, and salt. Mix and set aside.

3. Roughly chop the apples, add to the food processor, and pulse-blend until the apples are finely minced. If you don't have a food processor, leave the apples whole and use a cheese grater to shred them. You can also substitute unsweetened apple sauce.

4. In a separate mixing bowl, add the peeled bananas and mash them with a fork or potato masher; leave a few chunks. Then, add the apples, maple syrup, lemon juice, vanilla, and water. Stir to combine.

5. Add the wet mixture to the dry mixture; make sure they are well combined. Fill each section of the muffin tin all the way to the top. Because these muffins are so dense and don't contain flour, they don't rise much. So, you don't have to worry about them overflowing.

6. Bake for 30 to 35 minutes until the tops are golden brown. Use a toothpick as a tester by inserting it into the center of a muffin. When it comes out clean the muffins are ready. Let sit for 5 minutes, then transfer the muffins to a wire rack for 5 minutes. Leftover muffins can be kept in the refrigerator for up to a week and enjoyed cold or warm.

Real Southern Vegan Cornbread

Here in the South, we value our cornbread, and we don't accept cheap imitations. I can honestly say this recipe rivals even my grandmother's recipe. The combination of cornmeal, flour, and other ingredients creates a delectable, moist bread that pairs perfectly with soups and stews, or is simply enjoyed on its own. Get ready to experience southern hospitality at its finest.

1 cup (140 g) yellow cornmeal

1¼ cups (157 g) whole wheat flour or organic unbleached flour

1 tablespoon (14 g) baking powder

½ teaspoon (3 g) salt

¼ cup (80 g) maple syrup or agave nectar

1¼ cups (285 ml) unsweetened almond milk

1 tablespoon (15 ml) apple cider vinegar

⅓ cup (75 g) vegan butter, melted

Makes 1 pan, 8 x 8 x 2-inch (20 x 20 x 5-cm)

1. Preheat oven to 400°F (200°C) and line an 8 x 8 x 2-inch (20 x 20 x 5-cm) baking pan with parchment paper. You could also use a nonstick or silicone baking pan.

2. Combine the cornmeal, flour, baking powder, and salt in a large mixing bowl and whisk everything together. Add the maple syrup or agave nectar, almond milk, apple cider vinegar, and melted vegan butter to the dry mix. Stir the mixture until everything is combined, but *do not overmix*.

3. Pour the batter into the baking pan and bake for 25 to 30 minutes. The cornbread is done when you insert a toothpick into the middle and it comes out clean.

4. Remove from the oven, let the cornbread cool for a few minutes, and serve.

Fruity Breakfast Muffins

These are the ultimate healthy breakfast muffins: delicious, with an amazing aroma, and full of raisins, apples, and carrots. Nothing but pure wholesome goodness to start your day and have you shouting "Hallelujah" as you head off to work.

1½ tablespoons (11 g) flax meal

¼ cup (60 ml) water, warm

2¼ cups (216 g) whole wheat pastry flour

2½ teaspoons (11.5 g) baking soda

2 teaspoons (4 g) ground cinnamon

1 teaspoon (6 g) salt

½ cup (75 g) raisins

½ cup (60 g) chopped walnuts

2 teaspoons (4 g) ground ginger

1 cup (322 g) maple syrup

½ cup (100 g) organic cane sugar

1 cup (235 ml) unsweetened almond milk

¼ cup + 2 tablespoons (90 g) unsweetened applesauce

1½ cups (165 g) grated carrot

1 small apple, grated

Makes 12 muffins

1. Preheat your oven to 350°F (180°C). Line a muffin tin with liners, or oil them lightly.

2. Mix the flax meal and warm water together; set the mixture aside to let it gel. This will create a flax egg.

3. In a large mixing bowl, whisk together the flour, baking soda, cinnamon, and salt. Stir in the raisins, walnuts, and ginger.

4. In a separate bowl, whisk together the maple syrup, sugar, almond milk, and applesauce. Stir in the flax egg.

5. Fold the wet ingredients into the dry until everything is well incorporated, and then fold in the carrot and apple.

6. Portion out the batter into the muffin pan. Bake for 25 minutes, or until a toothpick inserted into the muffins comes out clean. Allow them to cool before enjoying.

TIPS & SUBS:

If you want a less-sweet muffin, use half the amount of sugar. You can also use date paste in place of maple syrup.

See page 44 for Sassy Sweet Potato Biscuits recipe

Biscuits, Buns, and Rolls

Deep South Homemade Biscuits

If you're looking for a delightful and cruelty-free twist on classic biscuits, this recipe for vegan homemade biscuits is just what you need. Made with simple plant-based ingredients, these biscuits are light, fluffy, and incredibly delicious. Get ready to savor the warm, buttery goodness that awaits you in each bite.

1 cup (235 ml) unsweetened soy milk

1 tablespoon (15 ml) apple cider vinegar

2½ cups (313 g) organic unbleached all-purpose flour, plus more as needed

2 tablespoons (27.6 g) baking powder

1 tablespoon (13 g) organic cane sugar

½ teaspoon (3 g) salt

½ cup (112 g) vegan butter, cold

Makes 10 to 12 biscuits

1. Preheat your oven to 425°F (220°C) and line a baking sheet with parchment paper.

2. In a small glass bowl, whisk together the soy milk and apple cider vinegar. Let it sit for a few minutes to curdle and create a vegan buttermilk substitute.

3. In a large mixing bowl, whisk together the flour, baking powder, sugar, and salt.

4. Add the cold vegan butter to the dry ingredients. Using a pastry cutter or your hands, cut the butter into the flour until the mixture resembles coarse crumbs or little pebbles.

5. Make a well in the center of the flour mixture and pour in the buttermilk mixture. Gently stir with a wooden spoon or spatula until the dough comes together. Do not overmix; it's okay if there are still some lumps.

6. Sprinkle a little flour onto a clean surface and transfer the dough onto it. Lightly knead the dough for about 1 to 2 minutes until it becomes smooth and cohesive. Roll out the dough to a thickness of about 1 inch (2.5 cm). Use a biscuit cutter or a glass to cut out biscuits from the dough. Press straight down without twisting to ensure the biscuits rise evenly.

7. Place the biscuits onto the prepared baking sheet so they are touching. This will help them bake up tall. Gather any remaining dough scraps and gently reroll and cut more biscuits until all the dough is used. You should be able to get 10 to 12 biscuits all together.

8. Bake the biscuits in the preheated oven for 12 to 15 minutes or until they turn golden brown on top. Remove the biscuits from the oven and let them cool on a wire rack for a few minutes before serving.

NOTES AND TIPS:

Melt some extra vegan butter and brush the tops of the biscuits before baking to make them even more golden.

Cover any of the leftover biscuits and store them at room temperature for up to 3 to 4 days. You can store them longer in the fridge or freeze them for up to 3 months.

Sassy Sweet Potato Biscuits

These sweet potato biscuits offer a delectable twist on the classic biscuit recipe. Whether you're hosting a brunch, preparing a cozy breakfast, or simply indulging in a delightful snack, these fluffy biscuits will surely impress. Enjoy with vegan butter, maple syrup, or plain and simple.

2 cups (250 g) organic unbleached all-purpose flour, plus more as needed

1 tablespoon (13.8 g) baking powder

¼ teaspoon (4 g) Morton's kosher salt

2 teaspoons (5 g) pumpkin pie spice

1 cup (225 g) mashed sweet potato, chilled (from about 1 large sweet potato)

¼ cup (60 ml) chilled cashew milk or full-fat coconut milk, plus more as needed

2 tablespoons (40 g) maple syrup

Makes 10 to 12 biscuits

1. Preheat your oven to 450°F (200°C) and line a baking sheet with parchment paper.

2. Whisk together the flour, baking powder, salt, and pumpkin pie spice in a large bowl.

3. In a small bowl, mix together the sweet potato, cashew or coconut milk, and maple syrup.

4. Pour the wet mixture into the dry ingredients and mix until the dough just comes together. Scrape the dough onto a lightly floured surface and use the heel of your hands to lightly press the dough together. If the dough seems a little dry and falls apart, add a little plant-based milk 1 tablespoon (15 ml) at a time. Usually, about 2 to 3 tablespoons (30 to 45 ml) should do it.

5. Flour your hands, add more flour to the surface if needed, and shape the dough into a rectangle that is about 1 inch (2.5 cm) thick.

6. Use a 2-inch (5-cm) biscuit cutter or glass to cut the dough. Press straight down without twisting to ensure the biscuits rise evenly. Place the biscuit rounds 1 inch (2.5 cm) apart on the baking sheet. Brush the tops with plant-based milk.

7. Place the biscuits in the oven for 10 to 12 minutes or until they rise and are just barely golden. Enjoy immediately or let them cool to room temperature.

Savory Spelt Drop Biscuits

Are you ready to create a biscuit that's both vegan and spelt-tacular? Well, hold onto your aprons! With their rustic charm and quirky irregular shapes, these biscuits are perfect for those who believe that imperfection is what gives life its flavor. So, gather your ingredients, embrace your inner biscuit artist, and let's whip up a batch of these slightly offbeat biscuits that will have everyone drooling and asking for seconds.

1 cup (235 ml) unsweetened plant-based milk, plus more as needed

1 tablespoon (15 ml) apple cider vinegar

1 cup (125 g) organic unbleached all-purpose flour

¾ cup (75 g) spelt flour

1 tablespoon (14 g) baking powder

2 teaspoons (2 g) Italian seasoning

1 teaspoon (6 g) sea salt

½ cup (112 g) chilled vegan butter

Makes 9 to 10 biscuits

1. Preheat oven at 450°F (230°C).

2. Make vegan buttermilk by whisking together the plant-based milk and apple cider vinegar in a small bowl. Set aside and allow to curdle.

3. To a large mixing bowl, add the flours, baking powder, Italian seasoning, and sea salt and whisk until well combined. Cut in the vegan butter until little pebbles form. Slowly and evenly stir in the vegan buttermilk. You can use a food processor to do this, but be sure not to overmix. The dough should be moist and sticky. If it seems dry, stir in a little more milk.

4. Drop large spoonfuls of dough about 1½ inches (3.5 cm) apart onto an ungreased baking sheet. Place the biscuits in the oven and bake for 12 to 15 minutes or until golden.

NOTES AND TIPS:

Be sure to measure your flour. Scoop it into a measuring cup and use the back of a knife to gently level the flour.

Don't overmix the dough. Once all of the dry flour is absorbed stop mixing.

Backyard Hamburger Buns

With their soft texture and delightful taste, these homemade buns will enhance the overall vegan burger experience and impress the heck out of everyone.

1 cup (235 ml) water, warm (around 110°F [43°C])

2 tablespoons (26 g) organic cane sugar

1 packet or 2¼ teaspoons (9 g) active dry yeast

3½ cups (420 g) organic unbleached all-purpose flour, plus more as needed

1 teaspoon (6 g) salt

¼ cup (60 ml) unsweetened plant-based milk, plus more as needed

2 tablespoons (28 g) vegan butter, melted

Sesame seeds (optional)

Makes 8 hamburger buns

1. In a small bowl, combine the warm water and sugar, stirring until the sugar dissolves. Sprinkle the yeast over the mixture and gently stir it in. Let it sit for about 10 minutes or until the mixture becomes foamy.

2. In a large mixing bowl, whisk together the flour and salt. Create a well in the center of the flour mixture and pour in the yeast mixture, plant-based milk, and melted vegan butter. Mix with a wooden spoon until a sticky dough forms.

3. Transfer the dough onto a lightly floured surface and knead it for 8 to 10 minutes. Add more flour, if necessary, but be careful not to add too much, as this can result in dense buns. The dough should become smooth and elastic.

4. Shape the dough into a ball and place it in a greased bowl, turning it to coat the surface. Cover the bowl with plastic wrap and let it rise in a warm, draft-free area for about 1 hour or until the dough has doubled in size.

5. Once the dough has risen, punch it down to release any air bubbles. Transfer it back to the floured surface and divide it into 8 equal portions. Roll each portion into a smooth ball and flatten it slightly with the palm of your hand. Place the buns on a baking sheet lined with parchment paper, leaving some space between them.

6. Cover the baking sheet with a damp kitchen towel and let the buns rise for another 30 to 45 minutes until they have doubled in size. Preheat your oven to 375°F (190°C).

7. If desired, brush the tops of the buns with a little plant-based milk and sprinkle with sesame seeds. Bake the buns for approximately 15 to 20 minutes or until they turn golden brown. Transfer the buns to a wire rack and allow them to cool completely before using.

Simple Vegan Hot Dog Buns

You only need six ingredients to make the best vegan hot dog buns. You no longer have to throw your money away on store-bought versions that are filled with chemicals and unhealthy ingredients. Fill these buns with my vegan carrot dogs (recipe on shaneandsimple.com), vegan sausages, or vegan cheesesteaks.

4 cups (480 g) bread flour, plus more as needed

1 packet or 2¼ teaspoons (7 g) instant yeast

¼ cup (50 g) organic cane sugar

1 teaspoon (6 g) salt

1½ cups (355 ml) water

¼ cup (55 g) vegan butter, melted (optional)

Makes 8 hot dog buns

1. Whisk together the flour, yeast, sugar, and salt in a large bowl. Pour in the water and use a wooden spoon to stir and fold the mixture until everything is mostly combined. If the mixture is sticky, then sprinkle in a little more flour.

2. Form a ball of dough using your hands. Once a ball is formed, clean and grease the same bowl, then place the dough ball back into the bowl. Cover the bowl with plastic wrap and let it sit for 90 minutes in a warm place.

3. Roll the dough out onto a lightly floured surface and cut the dough into 8 equal pieces. (If you want the buns to be the same size, it's best to use a food scale to weigh each piece.)

4. Form each piece of dough into a small loaf by folding the ends under, shaping it into a ball, and rolling it into a log. Line a baking sheet with parchment paper and place the dough in a line, approximately 1 inch (2.5 cm) apart. (This is so they grow together like store-bought when they bake.) Cover with a damp (not soaking wet!) towel. Let them sit for 1 hour in a warm place until doubled in size.

5. Remove the towel, brush each roll with the vegan butter if using, and bake at 375°F (190°C) for 25 to 35 minutes. Let cool for 10 minutes, then enjoy your homemade hot dog buns.

Brazilian Pão de Queijo *Cheese Rolls*

These small, chewy rolls are made with tapioca flour and vegan cheese, resulting in a delightful combination of cheesy, savory flavors and a unique texture that's both crispy on the outside and delightfully gooey on the inside. Perfect as a snack or appetizer, these vegan cheese rolls are sure to be a crowd-pleaser for everyone, regardless of their dietary preferences.

¼ cup (60 ml) aquafaba

3 tablespoons (45 ml) olive oil

3 tablespoons (45 g) vegan butter, melted

⅔ cup (160 ml) unsweetened plant-based milk

½ teaspoon (3 ml) white vinegar

1½ cups (170 g) tapioca flour

1 tablespoon (9 g) nutritional yeast

2 teaspoons (5 g) confectioner's sugar

1 teaspoon (5 g) baking powder

6 ounces (170 g) vegan mozzarella

1 teaspoon (6 g) salt

Makes 24 to 30 rolls

1. Preheat your oven to 400°F (200°C) and lightly grease two mini muffin pans.

2. Place all the aquafaba, olive oil, vegan butter, plant-based milk, white vinegar, tapioca flour, nutritional yeast, confectioner's sugar, baking powder, vegan mozzarella, and salt into a blender and pulse until smooth. Don't worry about overmixing the dough; there's no gluten in this recipe. Stop and scrape down the sides as needed so everything is thoroughly incorporated.

3. Once completely smooth, pour the batter into your prepared mini muffin pans so that they're filled three-quarters of the way to the top. Bake for 15 to 20 minutes, until the rolls are puffy and evenly browned all over. Remove from oven and let cool on a rack for 5 minutes. It's ok if some of them fall in the center as they cool. Serve right away and eat while still warm.

Better-Than-Deli Sandwich Rolls

These rolls are so fluffy and buttery, you will forget they are made without any animal products. Say goodbye to those awkward family dinners where you're stuck defending your plant-based choices—these rolls will have even the biggest carnivores begging for seconds.

1 cup (235 ml) warm water

1 tablespoon (13 g) organic cane sugar

1 packet or 2¼ teaspoons (9 g) active dry yeast

2 tablespoons (30 ml) olive oil

1 teaspoon (6 g) salt

3 cups (375 g) organic unbleached all-purpose flour

Makes 8 sandwich rolls

1. In a large mixing bowl, combine warm water and sugar. Sprinkle the yeast over the water and let it sit for about 5 minutes, or until foamy. Then, add the olive oil and salt to the yeast mixture and stir to combine.

2. Gradually add the flour to the mixture, stirring well after each addition. Once the dough becomes too thick to stir, transfer it to a floured surface and knead for about 5 to 7 minutes, or until smooth and elastic. Shape the dough into a ball and place it in a greased bowl. Cover the bowl with a clean kitchen towel and let the dough rise in a warm place for about 1 hour, or until it has doubled in size.

3. Preheat your oven to 400°F (200°C). Line a baking sheet with parchment paper.

4. Punch down the risen dough to release any air bubbles. Transfer the dough to a floured surface and divide it into 8 equal portions. Shape each portion by rolling it between your hands or gently stretching and tucking the dough underneath.

5. Place the rolls on the prepared baking sheet, leaving some space between them. Cover the rolls with a clean kitchen towel and let them rise for an additional 20 to 30 minutes.

6. Bake the rolls in the preheated oven for 15 to 20 minutes, or until golden brown and cooked through. Remove them from the oven and let them cool on a wire rack.

7. Once the rolls have cooled, slice them open and fill them with your favorite vegan sandwich fillings. Serve immediately or wrap tightly in plastic wrap to keep them fresh for later. Enjoy!

Gluten-Free Vegan Dinner Rolls

"Gluten-free and delicious? Can those words even coexist?" Well, my friend, prepare to be pleasantly surprised. These dinner rolls are here to prove that gluten-free doesn't mean flavor-free or crumbly. With their soft texture, irresistible aroma, and ability to hold your sandwich fillings without crumbling into a gluten-free mess, these rolls are a game-changer. So, get ready to unleash your inner gluten-free warrior, because today, we're breaking bread and breaking stereotypes with these mouthwatering vegan gluten-free dinner rolls.

3½ cups (546 g) gluten-free all-purpose flour

1 packet or 2¼ teaspoons (7 g) instant yeast

¼ cup (50 g) organic cane sugar

2 teaspoons (12 g) salt

2 teaspoons (9 g) baking powder

1½ cups (355 ml) unsweetened plant-based milk

¼ cup (55 g) + ⅓ cup (75 g) + ⅛ cup (75 g) vegan butter, melted, divided

½ cup (125 g) unsweetened applesauce

1 tablespoon (15 ml) apple cider vinegar

Cooking spray

Makes 15 dinner rolls

1. Add the gluten-free flour, instant yeast, sugar, salt, and baking powder to a large bowl and whisk everything together.

2. Pour in the unsweetened plant-based milk, ¼ cup (55 g) melted vegan butter, applesauce, and apple cider vinegar. If you have a stand mixer with a dough hook, you can use it to combine everything and bring the dough together. If you're mixing by hand, use a rubber spatula until everything is mixed well.

3. Once the dough is combined, remove it from the bowl and shape it into a ball. Spray the large glass bowl with cooking spray and place the dough ball back into the bowl. Cover the bowl with a clean dish towel and let it rise for 60 to 90 minutes or until it has doubled in size.

4. Once it has doubled, separate the dough into 15 equal pieces and roll each piece into a ball. Place each dough ball, seam-side down, on a greased 9 x 13-inch (23 x 33-cm) baking pan. Cover the pan and let the dough balls rise for 1 hour or until they have doubled in size. The balls should be touching after this rise; if not, let them rise a little longer.

5. Preheat your oven to 375°F (190°C) while the dough rises the second time and brush each roll liberally with ⅓ cup (75 g) melted butter. Place the baking pan in the oven and bake for 25 to 35 minutes or until the rolls are golden brown. Remove the rolls from the oven and brush with remaining ⅓ cup (75 g) melted butter.

Gettin' Lucky Dinner Rolls

When it comes to a satisfying and comforting meal, dinner rolls are the star of the show. Their soft texture and warm aroma make any dinner table feel complete. These decadent rolls are perfect to accompany soups, stews, or a hearty holiday feast. Give this recipe a try, and enjoy the satisfaction of baking your own dinner rolls from scratch.

1 cup (235 ml) unsweetened plant-based milk

2 tablespoons (26 g) organic cane sugar

1 packet or 2¼ teaspoons (7 g) instant yeast

3 cups (375 g) organic unbleached all-purpose flour, plus more as needed

1 teaspoon (6 g) salt

¼ cup (55 g) vegan butter, melted, plus more as needed

Sesame seeds or poppy seeds for topping, optional

Makes 12 rolls

1. In a small bowl, combine the plant-based milk and sugar. Warm the mixture in the microwave for about 30 seconds until it's lukewarm, but not too hot or it will kill the yeast. Sprinkle the yeast on top, give it a quick stir, and let it sit for about 5 minutes until it becomes frothy. If it doesn't foam, start over with new yeast.

2. In a large mixing bowl, whisk together the organic unbleached all-purpose flour and salt. Make a well in the center and pour in the activated yeast mixture along with the melted vegan butter.

3. Using a wooden spoon or your hands, mix the ingredients until they come together to form a dough. Transfer the dough to a lightly floured surface and knead it for about 5 to 7 minutes until it becomes smooth and elastic.

4. Place the dough in a lightly oiled bowl, cover it with a clean kitchen towel, and let it rise in a warm spot for approximately 1 to 1½ hours or until it has doubled in size.

5. Line a baking sheet with parchment. Once the dough has risen, punch it down gently to release any air bubbles. Transfer it to a lightly floured surface and divide it into 12 equal-sized portions. Shape each portion into a ball and place on the prepared baking sheet; leaving some space between the rolls, or they can be touching if you want that "pull-apart" effect.

6. Cover the rolls with a kitchen towel and let them rise for another 30 to 45 minutes until they have puffed up.

7. Meanwhile, preheat your oven to 375°F (190°C).

8. Once the rolls have risen, brush the tops with melted vegan butter and sprinkle sesame seeds or poppy seeds on top for added flavor and visual appeal, if desired. Bake them in the preheated oven for 15 to 20 minutes until they turn golden brown.

9. Remove the rolls from the oven and let them cool on a wire rack for a few minutes. Serve them warm with vegan butter or any spreads of your choice.

See page 65 for Plain Ol' White Bread recipe

CHAPTER
3

Everyday Loaves

Hometown Sourdough

Experience the satisfaction of making your own sourdough bread from scratch with this accessible and delicious recipe—it doesn't even require a starter! This recipe uses a clever combination of apple cider vinegar and a longer fermentation process to achieve that signature sourdough taste. With a crispy crust and a soft, airy interior, this bread is a testament to the wonders of plant-based baking.

4 cups (480 g) bread flour, plus more as needed

2 teaspoons (12 g) salt

1 packet or 2¼ teaspoons (7 g) instant yeast

1 tablespoon (15 ml) apple cider vinegar

2 cups (475 ml) water, warm (around 110°F [43°C])

Vegetable oil

Makes 1 round or oval loaf, 8 to 10 inches (20 to 25 cm) in diameter

1. In a large mixing bowl, whisk together the bread flour, salt, and instant yeast.

2. Create a well in the center of the dry ingredients and pour in the apple cider vinegar and warm water. Stir the mixture with a wooden spoon or your hands until a shaggy dough forms.

3. Cover the bowl with a clean kitchen towel and let it rest at room temperature for 30 minutes.

4. After 30 minutes, lightly oil your hands and fold the dough over itself a few times in the bowl. Cover again and let it rest for another 30 minutes.

5. Repeat the folding process 2 more times at 30-minute intervals. This will help to develop the gluten and strengthen the dough.

6. After the third folding, cover the bowl and let the dough rise for 8 to 12 hours at room temperature, or until it has doubled in size. You can also place it in the refrigerator for a longer, slower fermentation (up to 24 hours).

7. Preheat your oven to 450°F (230°C). Place a Dutch oven or a lidded oven-safe pot inside the oven to preheat as well.

8. When the dough has risen, carefully transfer it onto a lightly floured surface. Gently shape it into a round or oval loaf.

9. Carefully remove the preheated Dutch oven from the oven and place the dough inside. Score the top of the dough with a sharp knife or bread lame.

10. Cover the Dutch oven with the lid and place it back into the oven. Bake for 30 minutes.

11. Remove the lid from the Dutch oven and continue baking for an additional 15 to 20 minutes, or until the bread has a deep golden crust.

12. Once baked, remove the bread from the Dutch oven and let it cool on a wire rack before slicing.

Healthy Whole Wheat Sandwich Bread

This whole wheat sandwich bread is awesome! It combines the goodness of whole wheat with a pillowy, tender texture. This wholesome bread is perfect if you're seeking a healthier alternative to traditional white bread. You get more nutrition along with a soft and fluffy eating experience.

1¼ cups (285 ml) water, warm (around 110°F [43°C])

1½ teaspoons organic cane sugar (6 g) or maple syrup (10 g)

1½ teaspoons (5 g) active dry yeast

2 cups (250 g) whole wheat flour

1⅓ cups (167 g) organic unbleached all-purpose flour, plus more as needed

2 tablespoons (30 ml) olive oil

1½ teaspoons (9 g) salt

Makes one 8½ x 4½ x 2½-inch (21 x 11 x 6-cm) loaf

1. Whisk the water, sugar, and yeast together in a large mixing bowl. Let it sit for 5 minutes so the yeast can bloom.

2. Pour in the flours, oil, and salt, and mix with a wooden spoon until the dough comes together in a ball that does not stick to your fingers. If you have a stand mixer with a dough hook attachment, mix on low speed until the dough no longer sticks to the sides.

3. Transfer the dough to a lightly floured surface and knead the dough until it starts to form a tight ball. Grease a large glass mixing bowl, form the dough into a ball, and place it into the bowl. Roll the dough in the bowl so it is coated with oil. Cover the bowl with plastic wrap or a damp kitchen towel and set it in a warm place for 1 hour until the dough doubles in size. Save the plastic wrap or towel, as you'll be using it again.

4. Transfer the dough to a lightly floured surface and press it into a 7 x 7-inch (18 x 18-cm) square. *Do not roll it out!* Fold the top third of the square down and the bottom third up to form an even rectangle. Pinch the top fold and seal the dough.

5. Roll the dough over so the seam faces upward and fold both ends up toward the center, so the dough has formed an even log shape about the size of your 8½ x 4½ x 2½-inch (21 x 11 x 6-cm) loaf pan.

6. Spray the loaf pan with cooking spray, place the dough in the loaf pan, and cover with the plastic wrap or towel. Allow the dough rise for 1 hour, until it has proofed over the edge of the loaf pan 1 to 2 inches (2.5 to 5 cm).

7. Preheat the oven to 375°F (190°C). Remove the covering and bake for 50 to 55 minutes, until the dough has formed a light brown crust.

8. Immediately remove the bread from the pan and let it cool for at least 1 hour before slicing.

9. Store in an airtight container or bag or freeze it for up to 6 months.

NOTE:

Don't use all whole wheat flour because it won't be as fluffy. You'll get a very dense bread that doesn't rise as well.

Plain Ol' White Bread

Classic white bread is perfect for both sweet and savory toppings, making it an ideal choice for sandwiches, toast, or simply enjoyed on its own. With a light, airy texture and a crisp golden crust, vegan classic white bread offers a satisfying bite that caters to diverse dietary preferences while upholding the cherished qualities of traditional white bread.

3 cups bread flour (360 g) or organic unbleached all-purpose flour (375 g), plus more as needed

1 packet or 2¼ teaspoons (7 g) instant yeast

1 teaspoon (6 g) salt

1 tablespoon (13 g) organic cane sugar

1 cup (235 ml) water, warm (around 110°F [43°C])

2 tablespoons (30 ml) olive oil, plus more as needed

Makes one 9 x 5 x 3–inch (23 x 13 x 6-cm) loaf

1. In a large bowl, whisk together the flour, yeast, salt, and sugar. Add warm water and olive oil to the bowl and mix until the dough forms. Knead the dough for 5 to 10 minutes on a floured surface until it becomes smooth and elastic.

2. Place the dough in a lightly greased bowl and cover it with a damp cloth. Let it rise in a warm place for 1 hour or until it has doubled in size.

3. Preheat the oven to 350°F (180°C). Grease a 9 x 5 x 3-inch (23 x 13 x 6-cm) loaf pan.

4. Punch down the dough and shape it into a loaf that fits in the pan. Place the loaf into the prepared pan, cover it with a damp cloth, and let it rise for 30 minutes.

5. Bake the bread for 35 to 40 minutes or until the crust is golden brown. Remove the loaf from the pan. Hold it with a towel in one hand and give it a few quick knocks with your knuckles to check doneness. If it's done, it will sound hollow. If not, return the loaf to the pan and bake in 5- to 10-minute increments.

6. Remove the bread from the oven and let it cool in the pan for 5 minutes. Then, transfer it to a wire rack and let it cool completely before slicing.

TIPS:

To make a seeded bread, add ½ cup (77 g) of your favorite seeds to the dough before kneading.

For a softer crust, brush the loaf with melted vegan butter or oil right after it comes out of the oven.

To store the bread, wrap it in plastic wrap and store it in the refrigerator for up to 1 week.

Rustic Homemade Rye Bread

Bursting with hearty rye flavors and a satisfyingly dense texture, this homemade loaf showcases a perfect harmony of plant-based ingredients, including dark rye flour and a touch of molasses for a subtle sweetness. Baked to perfection, each slice delivers a nutty aroma and robust taste, making it an ideal companion for savory spreads or a simple yet gratifying snack; this delightful fusion of taste and nourishment will leave you craving more. If you're looking for ideas on how to enjoy this delicious bread, head over to shaneandsimple.com and try it with my vegan sweet potato Reuben sandwich.

2 cups (256 g) dark rye flour

1 cup (125 g) organic unbleached all-purpose flour, plus more as needed

1 teaspoon (6 g) salt

1 tablespoon (7 g) caraway seeds, plus more for sprinkling on top

1½ cups (355 ml) water, warm

2 tablespoons (40 g) molasses

1 packet or 2¼ teaspoons (9 g) active dry yeast

1 tablespoon (15 ml) olive oil

Makes 1 round or oval loaf, 10 inches (25 cm) in diameter

1. Whisk together the flours, salt, and caraway seeds in a medium-sized mixing bowl and set aside. In a large mixing bowl, combine the warm water and molasses and stir until the molasses is fully dissolved. Sprinkle the yeast over the water mixture and let it sit for about 5 minutes, or until it becomes foamy. Add the olive oil to the yeast mixture and stir well to combine.

2. Gradually add the dry ingredients to the wet ingredients, stirring with a wooden spoon or a dough hook attachment of a stand mixer. Continue mixing until a sticky dough forms.

3. Once the dough starts to come together, transfer it to a floured surface and knead for about 5 to 7 minutes, or until the dough becomes smooth and elastic. Add additional flour as needed to prevent sticking but be careful not to add too much.

4. Place the dough in a lightly greased bowl, cover it with a clean kitchen towel, and let it rise in a warm place for about 1 hour, or until it doubles in size. Preheat your oven to 400°F (200°C) and line a baking sheet with parchment paper.

5. Once the dough has risen, gently punch it down to release any air bubbles. Transfer it to the prepared baking sheet and shape it into a round or oval loaf. Using a sharp knife or bread lame, make a few diagonal slashes on the top of the loaf. This will allow the bread to expand while baking. Sprinkle some caraway seeds on top.

6. Place the baking sheet in the preheated oven and bake for about 35 to 40 minutes, or until the bread is golden brown. Remove the loaf from the sheet. Hold it with a towel in one hand and give it a few quick knocks with your knuckles to check doneness. If it's done, it will sound hollow. If not, return the loaf to the sheet and bake in 5- to 10-minute increments. Remove the bread from the oven and let it cool completely on a wire rack before slicing.

Oil-Free Perfect Pumpernickel

When it comes to hearty and flavorful bread, pumpernickel stands out with its distinctive dark color and rich taste. The combination of dark rye flour, wholesome ingredients, and aromatic seeds creates a loaf that is rich in flavor whether fresh or toasted, and is perfect for pairing with spreads or using as a foundation for sandwiches.

1¾ cups (425 ml) water, warm (around 110°F [43°C])

1 tablespoon (20 g) molasses

1 tablespoon (20 g) maple syrup

1 packet or 2¼ teaspoons (7 g) instant yeast

2 cups (256 g) dark rye flour

1½ cups (188 g) whole wheat flour

½ cup (63 g) organic unbleached all-purpose flour, plus more as needed

1½ teaspoons (9 g) salt

1 teaspoon (2 g) cocoa powder

2 teaspoons (4 g) caraway seeds

1 teaspoon (2 g) fennel seeds

1 teaspoon (2 g) coriander seeds

Cornmeal for dusting

Makes 1 rectangular loaf, 8 to 10 slices

1. In a small bowl, combine the warm water, molasses, and maple syrup. Sprinkle the instant yeast over the mixture and let it sit for about 5 minutes until it becomes foamy.

2. In a large mixing bowl, combine the flours, salt, cocoa powder, caraway seeds, fennel seeds, and coriander seeds. Stir until the ingredients are well mixed.

3. Pour the yeast mixture into the dry ingredients. Mix well with a wooden spoon or your hands until the dough comes together.

4. Transfer the dough onto a lightly floured surface. Knead for about 10 minutes, adding more flour as needed, until the dough becomes smooth and elastic.

5. Place the dough in a greased bowl and cover it with a clean kitchen towel. Allow it to rise in a warm place for about 1 to 1½ hours, or until it doubles in size.

6. After the dough has risen, gently punch it down to release any air bubbles. Shape it into a loaf by rolling it tightly from one end and pinching the seams together. Place the loaf on a baking sheet dusted with cornmeal. Cover the loaf with a towel and let it rise again for about 30 to 45 minutes, until it has visibly increased in size. Meanwhile, preheat your oven to 375°F (190°C).

7. Once the second rise is complete, remove the towel and slash the top of the loaf with a sharp knife or bread lame. This helps to release steam during baking. Bake the bread for approximately 40 to 45 minutes. Remove the loaf from the sheet. Hold it with a towel in one hand and give it a few quick knocks with your knuckles to check doneness. If it's done, it will sound hollow. If not, return the loaf to the sheet and bake in 5- to 10-minute increments.

8. When it has finished baking, transfer the pumpernickel bread to a wire rack and allow it to cool completely before slicing.

Soft Wheat Sandwich Bread

Are you tired of healthy bread that tastes like cardboard, but think making bread is like some lost mystical art? If you have 5 ingredients, a pair of hands, and just a little bit of time, then you can make this healthy and delicious whole wheat bread. And, best of all, you don't need to knead.

4 cups (500 g) whole wheat flour

1 packet or 2¼ teaspoons (7 g) instant yeast

½ teaspoon (3 g) salt

1 tablespoon (20 g) maple syrup

2 cups (475 ml) water, warm (around 110°F [43°C])

Cooking spray

Makes one 9 x 5 x 3-inch (23 x 13 x 6-cm) loaf

1. Add the flour to a mixing bowl with the yeast and salt and mix together.

2. Dissolve the maple syrup in the warm water and then add it to the dry ingredients.

3. Mix—don't knead—until you have a sticky, well-combined dough.

4. Grease a 9 x 5 x 3-inch (23 x 13 x 6-cm) loaf pan. You can also line the bottom with parchment paper if you think there will be any chance of it sticking. Transfer the dough to the pan. Cover and leave to rise for 20 minutes.

5. While the dough is rising, preheat the oven to 390°F (200°C).

6. Bake in the oven for 40 minutes.

TIPS:

This bread is best when fresh because there are no preservatives to keep it around for 100 years. However, it will keep for a couple of days in a closed container, and it makes excellent croutons and toast. Freeze it the day you bake it if you want to keep it around for a while.

Wicked Awesome Anadama Bread

Anadama is a traditional bread that originated in New England. According to legend, anadama bread was invented in Rockport, Massachusetts, in the 19th century. The story goes that a fisherman was frustrated with his monotonous diet of cornmeal mush. One day, he combined these ingredients with molasses and flour, creating a simple yet delicious bread. He called it "Anna, damn her" bread, expressing his frustration with his wife's inability to cook a varied meal. Regardless of its origins, anadama bread has a hearty and slightly sweet taste, making it a popular choice for sandwiches, toast, or simply enjoyed on its own. The bread itself has become a beloved part of New England culinary tradition, and variations of the recipe can be found in cookbooks and bakeries throughout the region.

1½ cups (210 g) cornmeal

1½ cups (188 g) whole wheat flour

1½ cups (188 g) organic unbleached all-purpose flour, plus more as needed

1 packet or 2¼ teaspoons (7 g) instant yeast

1½ teaspoons (9 g) salt

1¾ cups (425 ml) water, warm (around 110°F [43°C])

⅓ cup (114 g) molasses

2 tablespoons (30 ml) vegetable oil, plus extra for greasing

Makes one 9 x 5 x 3-inch (23 x 13 x 6-cm) loaf

1. In a large mixing bowl, combine the cornmeal, whole wheat flour, organic unbleached all-purpose flour, instant yeast, and salt. Mix well.

2. In a separate bowl, whisk together the warm water, molasses, and vegetable oil until well combined.

3. Make a well in the center of the dry ingredients and pour the wet mixture into it. Stir with a wooden spoon until the dough comes together.

4. Transfer the dough to a lightly floured surface and knead for about 5 to 7 minutes, until the dough becomes smooth and elastic.

5. Grease a clean mixing bowl with vegetable oil and place the dough in it. Cover the bowl with a clean kitchen towel and let the dough rise in a warm place for about 1 to 1½ hours, or until it has doubled in size.

6. Once the dough has risen, gently punch it down to release any air pockets. Transfer the dough to a lightly floured surface and shape it into a loaf.

7. Grease a 9 x 5 x 3-inch (23 x 13 x 6-cm) loaf pan with vegetable oil and place the shaped dough into the pan. Cover the pan with the kitchen towel and let it rise for another 30 to 45 minutes.

8. Preheat the oven to 375°F (190°C).

9. Once the dough has risen again, place the loaf pan in the preheated oven and bake for approximately 30 to 35 minutes, or until the bread is golden brown. Remove the loaf from the pan. Hold it with a towel in one hand and give it a few quick knocks with your knuckles to check doneness. If it's done, it will sound hollow. If not, return the loaf to the pan and bake in 5- to 10-minute increments.

10. Remove the bread from the oven and let it cool in the pan for 5 minutes. Then transfer the bread to a wire rack and let it cool completely before slicing.

NOTE:
This is perfect for toast and excellent for topping with your favorite nut butter.

No Yeast Bread

This yeastless bread is delicious and so easy to make. All you need is 1 bowl and 3 simple pantry staple ingredients. It's perfect when you need bread in a hurry: No yeast. No proofing. No oil.

4 cups (500 g) organic unbleached all-purpose flour, plus more as needed

1 tablespoon (14 g) baking powder

¾ teaspoon (5 g) salt

1 tablespoon (15 g) unsweetened applesauce

1⅔ cups (395 ml) water

Makes 1 round or oval loaf, 8 to 10 inches (20 to 25 cm) in diameter

1. Preheat your oven to 375°F (190°C).

2. Add flour, baking powder, and salt to a large mixing bowl and whisk until everything is well combined.

3. Add the applesauce and water to the dry mixture. Using the handle of a wooden spoon, begin stirring everything together until most or all of the wet ingredients are absorbed. Then, use your hands to knead the dough until the texture is consistent.

4. Lightly flour a baking stone or pizza pan lined with parchment paper. Lay out the dough, form it into a circular shape, and flatten it until it is about 1 to 1½ inches (2.5 to 4 cm) thick. If it is thicker than that, it will not bake all the way through.

5. Use a sharp knife or bread lame to make a large X in the top of the dough that is about ½ to ¾ an inch (1 to 2 cm) deep.

6. Bake the bread for 40 minutes or until done. The bread will have more of a homemade biscuit texture and will only brown slightly on the top and around the bottom edges. Remove the loaf from the stone or pan. Hold it with a towel in one hand and give it a few quick knocks with your knuckles to check doneness. If it's done, it will sound hollow. If not, return the loaf to the stone or pan and bake in 5- to 10-minute increments.

Vegan Irish Soda Bread

This rustic Irish soda bread is crusty and delicious. Made in 1 bowl with just 5 simple ingredients, it's so easy to make and ready in less than 30 minutes

2 cups (475 ml) oat milk

2 tablespoons (30 ml) white vinegar or apple cider vinegar

4 cups (500 g) organic unbleached flour or whole wheat flour, plus more as needed

2 teaspoons (9 g) baking soda

½ teaspoon (3 g) salt

1 cup (145 g) raisins

Makes 1 round loaf, 8 to 10 inches (20 to 25 cm) in diameter

1. Place an oven rack in the center of the oven and preheat your oven to 430°F (220°C) and line a baking sheet with parchment paper.

2. Add the milk and vinegar to a bowl, whisk, and let it sit for a few minutes. This will give the milk time to curdle and will create a vegan buttermilk substitute.

3. To a large mixing bowl, add the flour, baking soda, and salt; whisk together. Create a well in the center and pour in the vegan buttermilk.

4. Begin to mix the dough with a wooden spoon or spatula, then use your hands to knead the dough when it becomes more difficult to mix. Fold in the raisins.

5. Knead the dough inside the mixing bowl for a couple of minutes until you can form a ball. If the dough is wet and sticky, add a little more flour. Be careful not to add too much. If the dough is too dry, your bread will turn out dry and dense. You want the dough to be a little sticky so you get a more moist bread.

6. Transfer the dough to the baking sheet with parchment paper; flatten the dough into a disc until it's about ½ to 1 inch (1 to 2.5 cm) thick. The thickness is important. Because there is no yeast in this bread, if it's too flat, it won't rise. If it's too thick, it won't rise as well either. Then, use a serrated knife or bread lame to cut an X on top of the dough. Sprinkle a little extra flour on top.

7. Place in the oven on the center rack and bake for 25 to 30 minutes until it's golden, crusty, and cooked all the way through.

8. Remove the bread from the oven, transfer to a cooling rack, and let the bread cool for at least 1 hour before slicing.

TIPS:

Don't overknead. You only want to knead the dough until you can form a ball. Too much mixing will cause the bread to be extremely dense once it's baked.

This bread is perfect for freezing. It will keep for up to 3 months frozen.

Happy Hour Beer Bread

Beer ain't just for drinkin' . . . it also makes amazing bread! Here is an easy five-ingredient whole wheat beer bread that's fat-free and super simple to make. It is crunchy on the outside, soft and chewy on the inside, and purely delicious.

3 cups whole wheat pastry flour (288 g) or whole wheat flour (375 g)

1 tablespoon (13.8 g) baking powder

1 teaspoon (6 g) salt

3 tablespoons (60 g) maple syrup

12-ounce (355 ml) bottle of your favorite beer (I prefer a darker beer like Guinness or Newcastle)

Oil or cooking spray

Makes one 8½ x 4½ x 2½-inch (21 x 11 x 6-cm) loaf

1. Preheat your oven to 375°F (190°C).

2. In a mixing bowl, add the flour, baking powder, and salt; whisk the ingredients together.

3. Add the maple syrup along with the beer and mix with a wooden spoon until a dough forms and everything is well combined. Use your hands if needed.

4. Grease a 8½ x 4½ x 2½-inch (21 x 11 x 6-cm) loaf pan and scrape the dough into the pan.

5. Bake for 45 to 55 minutes. Check to see if the bread is done by inserting a knife in the center. If it comes out clean, the bread is done.

Herbed Pull-Apart Bread

Get ready from something truly amazing! This pull-apart bread is a true crowd-pleaser, making it the perfect addition to any meal or gathering. With its enticing aroma, crispy exterior, and soft, buttery interior, it's a treat that will have everyone reaching for seconds. Whether you're a bread enthusiast or simply looking to elevate your culinary skills, this recipe is guaranteed to satisfy.

¾ cup (175 ml) water, warm (around 110°F [43°C])

1 packet or 2¼ teaspoons (7 g) active dry yeast

¼ cup (55 g) vegan butter, melted, plus more as needed

2½ cups (313 g) organic unbleached all-purpose flour, plus more as needed

1 teaspoon (1 g) Italian seasoning

1 teaspoon (2 g) garlic powder

1 teaspoon (6 g) salt

6 tablespoons (90 g) salted vegan butter, softened

6 cloves garlic, finely minced

Makes one 8½ x 4½ x 2½-inch (21 x 11 x 6-cm) loaf

1. Add the water and yeast to a large mixing bowl and let it sit 5 to 10 minutes so the yeast will activate. Then, add in the melted vegan butter and mix. Add the flour, Italian seasoning, garlic powder, and salt; mix until a thick and shaggy dough forms.

2. Once the dough has formed, transfer to a well-floured surface and knead for 8 to 10 minutes. When the dough is smooth and tacky, but not super sticky, it's time to stop kneading. It should be able to easily stretch without the dough tearing. Form the dough into a round ball and place it into a well-oiled bowl. Cover the bowl with a clean kitchen towel for 1 hour until the dough has doubled in size.

3. While the dough is rising, go ahead and make the garlic butter. Add the softened butter and minced garlic to a bowl and mash together until smooth.

4. Line an 8½ x 4½ x 2½-inch (21 x 11 x 6-cm) loaf pan with parchment paper. Once the dough has doubled in size, punch it down to remove excess air and remove it from the bowl. Dump it on a well-floured surface and divide it into 10 to 12 evenly sized pieces.

5. Roll each section of dough into a round ball. Use your hands or a rolling pin to flatten each ball into a circular disc. Don't worry if it's not perfectly round; that's not important. Spread 1 to 2 teaspoons (5 to 9 g) of the garlic butter filling onto each dough circle, then fold in half and line them in the prepared baking pan with the curved side up.

6. Cover the loaf pan with a clean kitchen towel and let it rise another 30 minutes. Uncover the bread and preheat your oven to 350°F (180°C). Brush the bread with some of the melted butter before baking so the crust will brown.

7. Place the bread in the oven and bake for 40 to 50 minutes until the top starts to brown and the bread has cooked through.

8. Take the bread out of the oven and let it cool in the pan for 5 to 10 minutes. Then, take the bread out of the loaf pan and set it onto a wire rack to cool. Eat by pulling apart; enjoy!

Gluten-Free Sandwich Bread

This recipe is perfect for anyone on a gluten-free diet or looking to enjoy a delicious and healthy homemade bread. Made with a combination of gluten-free flours, it yields a soft and fluffy loaf that's ideal for sandwiches or toast—better yet, there's no reason to knead this bread dough because there's not gluten to activate. Roll up your sleeves and get ready to bake a delightful loaf that will satisfy all your bread cravings!

2 cups (312 g) gluten-free all-purpose flour

1 cup (128 g) brown rice flour

½ cup (57 g) tapioca flour

2 tablespoons (14 g) ground flaxseed

1 packet or 2¼ teaspoons (7 g) instant yeast

1 teaspoon (6 g) salt

1½ cups (355 ml) water, warm (around 110°F [43°C])

2 tablespoons (40 g) maple syrup or agave nectar

2 tablespoons (30 ml) olive oil

Makes one 8½ x 4½ x 2½-inch (21 x 11 x 6-cm) loaf

1. In a large mixing bowl, combine the flours, ground flaxseed, yeast, and salt. Mix well to ensure even distribution of ingredients.

2. Create a well in the center of the dry ingredients and pour in the warm water, maple syrup or agave nectar, and olive oil. Stir everything together with a wooden spoon until a sticky dough forms.

3. Grease or line an 8½ x 4½ x 2½-inch (21 x 11 x 6-cm) bread loaf pan with parchment. Transfer the dough to the pan, smoothing out the top with a spatula or wet hands. Cover the pan with a clean kitchen towel and let the dough rise in a warm place for about 1 hour or until it doubles in size. This process may take longer depending on the temperature.

4. Preheat the oven to 375°F (190°C) while the dough is rising. When the dough has risen, place the loaf pan in the preheated oven. Bake for 35 to 40 minutes or until the bread is golden brown. Remove the loaf from the pan. Hold it with a towel in one hand and give it a few quick knocks with your knuckles to check doneness. If it's done, it will sound hollow. If not, return the loaf to the pan and bake in 5- to 10-minute increments.

5. Remove the bread from the oven and allow it to cool in the pan for 10 minutes. Then, transfer the loaf to a wire rack to cool completely before slicing.

6. Once the bread has cooled, slice it and enjoy as desired! It's perfect for sandwiches, toast, or any other bread-based creation you can think of.

NOTE:
Store any leftover bread in an airtight container or bag to maintain its freshness. You can also freeze slices for longer storage.

See page 84 for Awesome Freakin' Focaccia recipe

Artisan and European Breads

Very Veneto Ciabatta Bread

Ciabatta bread, with its rustic crust and soft, airy interior, is a staple in Italian cuisine. While traditional ciabatta recipes contain eggs and milk, veganizing this delightful bread is simple. By substituting a few plant-based ingredients, you can create a vegan ciabatta that is just as delicious and satisfying. Serve your freshly baked ciabatta with your favorite spreads or use it to make sandwiches or bruschetta.

1½ cups (355 ml) water, warm (around 110°F [43°C])

1 tablespoon (13 g) organic cane sugar

1 packet or 2¼ teaspoons (7 g) instant yeast

4 cups (500 g) organic unbleached all-purpose flour, plus more as needed

2 teaspoons (12 g) salt

2 tablespoons (30 ml) olive oil, plus more as needed

Makes 2 rectangular loaves, about 10 x 4 inches (25 x 10 cm)

1. In a small bowl, combine the warm water and sugar. Stir until the sugar is dissolved. Sprinkle the instant yeast over the water and let it sit for about 5 minutes until it becomes frothy. This indicates that the yeast is active and ready to use.

2. In a large mixing bowl, combine the flour and salt. Make a well in the center of the dry ingredients and pour in the activated yeast mixture and olive oil. Stir the mixture with a wooden spoon until it comes together and forms a shaggy dough.

3. Transfer the dough to a lightly floured surface and knead for about 8 to 10 minutes, or until it becomes smooth and elastic. If the dough is too sticky, you can add a little extra flour, but be careful not to add too much.

4. Place the dough in a clean, lightly oiled bowl and cover it with a kitchen towel. Allow it to rise in a warm place for approximately 1 to 1½ hours, or until it has doubled in size.

5. After the dough has risen, gently deflate it by pressing down with your hands. Transfer it to a floured surface and divide it into 2 equal portions. Shape each portion into a rectangular shape about 10 inches long and 4 inches wide (25 x 10 cm).

6. Place the shaped dough onto a parchment-lined baking sheet. Cover it with a kitchen towel and let it rise for another 30 to 45 minutes, or until it has increased in size.

7. While the dough is undergoing its second rise, preheat your oven to 450°F (230°C).

8. Once the dough has risen again, lightly dust the loaves with flour and use a sharp knife or a bread lame to make diagonal slashes on the surface. This will allow the bread to expand while baking. Place the baking sheet in the preheated oven and bake for 20 to 25 minutes, or until the bread is golden brown. Remove the loaves from the sheet. Hold each with a towel in one hand and give it a few quick knocks with your knuckles to check doneness. If it's done, it will sound hollow. If not, return the loaf to the sheet and bake in 5- to 10-minute increments.

9. Remove the ciabatta from the oven and transfer them to a wire rack to cool completely. Allow to cool for at least 20 to 30 minutes before slicing. Serve your freshly baked vegan ciabatta with your favorite spreads or use it to make sandwiches or bruschetta.

Awesome Freakin' Focaccia

Focaccia, with its light and fluffy texture, aromatic herbs, and satisfyingly crispy crust is a beloved Italian bread that pairs perfectly with soups, salads, or as a stand-alone snack. Let me guide you through this simple recipe that will surely become a favorite in your kitchen.

1 cup (235 ml) water, warm (around 110°F [43°C])

1 teaspoon (4 g) organic cane sugar

1 packet or 2¼ teaspoons (9 g) active dry yeast

3 cups (375 g) organic unbleached all-purpose flour, plus more as needed

1 teaspoon (6 g) salt

2 tablespoons (30 ml) olive oil, plus more as needed

1 tablespoon (3 g) Italian seasoning

1 teaspoon (6 g) coarse sea salt

Optional toppings of choice: Cherry tomatoes, sun-dried tomatoes, olives

Makes 1 rectangular loaf, 18 x 13 inch (46 x 23 cm) or 13 x 9 inch (33 x 23 cm)

1. In a small bowl, combine warm water, sugar, and yeast. Stir gently and set aside for around 5 to 10 minutes until it becomes frothy.

2. In a large mixing bowl, combine the organic unbleached all-purpose flour and salt. Make a well in the center and pour in the activated yeast mixture along with the olive oil. Mix everything together until it forms a shaggy dough.

3. Transfer the dough onto a clean and lightly floured surface. Knead the dough for about 5 to 7 minutes until it becomes smooth and elastic. If the dough feels too sticky, add a little more flour.

4. Grease a large bowl with olive oil and place the dough inside. Cover the bowl with a clean kitchen towel or plastic wrap and let the dough rise in a warm spot for approximately 1 to 2 hours or until it doubles in size.

5. Once the dough has risen, gently punch it down to release the air. Transfer it to a greased 18 x 13 inch (46 x 23 cm) baking sheet or a 13 x 9 x 2 inch (33 x 23 x 5 cm) rectangular baking dish. Press and stretch the dough to fit the size of your baking vessel. If desired, you can create dimples on the surface with your fingers.

6. Cover the shaped dough with the kitchen towel or plastic wrap and let it rise again for 30 to 45 minutes. Meanwhile, preheat your oven to 425°F (220°C).

7. Drizzle the top of the dough with olive oil and spread it evenly. Sprinkle the Italian seasoning and coarse sea salt over the surface. If desired, you can add cherry tomatoes, sun-dried tomatoes, olives, or any other toppings you prefer.

8. Place the focaccia in the preheated oven and bake for 20 to 25 minutes or until it turns golden brown and the crust becomes crispy. Keep an eye on it to prevent burning.

9. Once the focaccia is baked, remove it from the oven and let it cool for a few minutes. Transfer it to a wire rack to cool completely or enjoy it warm. Slice it into squares or wedges and serve it alongside your favorite dips or soups.

See photo page 80 for this recipe

One-Hour Olive and Roasted Garlic Bread

Breadmaking is an ancient craft that requires time, patience, and skill. No-knead or "Dutch oven" breads are perfect, with an excellent crust and a light and airy crumb inside. The dough has to rest overnight, but no kneading is necessary. Get ready for an amazing experience with this mouthwatering flavor combo.

1 head of garlic

Olive oil for roasting garlic

3 cups (375 g) organic unbleached all-purpose flour, plus more as needed

1½ teaspoons (9 g) salt

Generous ¼ teaspoon (1 g) of active dry yeast

1 cup (100 g) pitted and chopped olives

1½ cups (355 ml) water, room temperature

Makes 1 round loaf, 8 to 10 inches (20 to 25 cm) in diameter

1. Preheat your oven to 400°F (200°C). Cut off the top of the garlic head to expose the cloves. Drizzle olive oil over the garlic, wrap it in aluminum foil, and place it in the oven. Roast for about 30 minutes or until the cloves become soft and golden. Allow the head to cool, then squeeze out the roasted garlic cloves.

2. In a large bowl, combine the flour, salt, and yeast. Add the chopped olives and roasted garlic cloves to the dry ingredients. Slowly pour in the water. Using a wooden spoon or your hands, mix the ingredients until they come together into a shaggy, sticky dough. Avoid overmixing; a few lumps and uneven textures are normal.

3. Cover the bowl with plastic wrap or a damp kitchen towel and let it rest at room temperature for 12 to 18 hours. This lengthy fermentation process will develop the bread's flavor and create air pockets in the dough.

4. After the long rise, the dough should be bubbly and doubled in size. Generously flour a clean surface and turn the dough out onto it. Fold the dough gently over itself a few times, shaping it into a round or oval loaf. Place the dough seam-side down on a sheet of parchment paper.

5. Cover the dough with a kitchen towel and let it rise for another 1 to 2 hours. During this time, the bread will undergo its final fermentation, becoming airier and more flavorful.

6. Preheat your oven to 450°F (230°C). Place a Dutch oven or a cast-iron pot with a lid into the oven while it preheats. This will create a steamy environment, allowing the bread to rise and develop a crisp crust. Carefully remove the preheated pot from the oven, lift the dough using the parchment paper, and place the paper and the dough into the pot. Score the top of the dough with a sharp knife or bread lame to allow for even expansion.

7. Cover the pot with the lid and return it to the oven. Bake for 30 minutes. Remove the lid and bake for an additional 15 to 20 minutes or until the bread has a deep golden crust. The internal temperature should reach around 200°F (93°C).

8. Once baked, remove the bread from the oven and carefully transfer it to a cooling rack. Allow it to cool for at least 30 minutes before slicing. The anticipation will be worth it when you finally savor the warm, aromatic slices of olive and roasted garlic bread.

Vegan Buttery Brioche

Brioche bread, with its rich, buttery texture and delicate sweetness, is a beloved staple in bakeries and kitchens around the world. Traditionally made with eggs and butter, this French classic might seem like a challenging task for vegans. But, with the right ingredients and techniques, you can create a vegan brioche bread that rivals its non-vegan counterpart and will leave you in awe of its fluffy texture and mouthwatering flavor. Let's do this!

1½ cups (355 ml) +
1 tablespoon (15 ml)
unsweetened almond
milk, divided

1 packet or 2¼
teaspoons (9 g) active
dry yeast

⅓ cup (75 g) vegan
butter, melted

⅓ cup (67 g) organic
cane sugar

4 cups (500 g) organic
unbleached all-purpose
flour, plus more as
needed

1 teaspoon (6 g) salt

2 tablespoons (40 g)
maple syrup

Cooking spray

Makes one 8½ x 4½ x 2½-inch (21 x 11 x 6-cm) loaf

1. Heat 1½ cups (355 ml) almond milk in a small saucepan over low heat until it reaches a lukewarm temperature (around 110°F [43°C]). Avoid overheating, as this may kill the yeast.

2. Sprinkle the yeast over the warm almond milk and add a pinch of sugar. Gently stir and set it aside for about 5 to 10 minutes until the yeast becomes foamy.

3. In a large mixing bowl, combine the yeast mixture, melted butter, sugar, flour, and salt. Stir with a wooden spoon until the ingredients are well combined and form a sticky dough.

4. Transfer the dough onto a lightly floured surface and knead it for about 8 to 10 minutes until it becomes smooth and elastic. Add a little extra flour if needed to prevent sticking.

5. Place the dough in a greased bowl, cover it with a clean kitchen towel or plastic wrap, and let it rise in a warm place for approximately 1 to 2 hours or until it doubles in size.

6. Once the dough has risen, gently punch it down to release the air. Divide the dough into 3 equal-sized portions and shape them into balls. Roll each of them into 12- to 14-inch (30- to 36-cm) logs. Braid the logs and tuck the ends under to make them tidy.

7. Spray an 8½ x 4½ x 2½-inch (21 x 11 x 6-cm) loaf pan with cooking spray and place the braided loaf in the pan. Lightly spray the top of the dough and a piece of plastic wrap; cover the dough and let it rise for at least 2 hours until it puffs up or doubles in size. *Be sure to oil the plastic wrap and the top of the bread. If the plastic wrap tears the dough, it will deflate.*

8. Preheat your oven to 350°F (180°C). In a small bowl, whisk together the maple syrup and 1 tablespoon (15 ml) almond milk to create the glaze. Brush the glaze gently over the risen dough to give it a beautiful golden shine.

9. Place the brioche bread in the preheated oven and bake for 20 to 25 minutes or until the top turns golden brown. Keep an eye on it to avoid overbrowning.

10. Once the vegan brioche bread is baked to perfection, remove it from the oven and let it cool on a wire rack. Slice it and enjoy the fluffy, buttery, and delectable vegan brioche goodness!

Simple Spelt & Oat Bread

This wholesome bread is packed with nutrients, fiber, and rustic delicious flavors. Spelt flour offers a notable benefit as a nutritious and flavorful alternative to traditional wheat flour. It imparts a distinct, nutty flavor to baked goods, adding a delightful depth to recipes. This wholesome and ancient grain flour provides a wonderful option for those seeking a healthier and more diverse culinary experience while still enjoying the familiar satisfaction of baked treats.

2 cups (198 g) spelt flour, plus more as needed

1 cup (92 g) oat flour

1 cup (80 g) rolled oats

1 packet or 2¼ teaspoons (9 g) active dry yeast

1 teaspoon (6 g) salt

1¼ cups (285 ml) water, warm (around 110°F [43°C])

1 tablespoon (20 g) maple syrup or agave nectar

2 tablespoons (30 ml) olive oil

Rolled oats for topping (optional)

Makes one 8½ x 4½ x 2½-inch (21 x 11 x 6-cm) loaf

1. In a large mixing bowl, combine the flours, rolled oats, yeast, and salt. Mix well.

2. In a separate bowl, mix together the warm water and maple syrup (or agave nectar) until the sweetener is dissolved. Add the olive oil and mix again.

3. Pour the wet ingredients into the dry ingredients and stir with a wooden spoon until a sticky dough forms. Transfer the dough to a floured surface and knead for about 5 to 7 minutes until the dough becomes smooth and elastic. If the dough is too sticky, you can add a little more spelt flour.

4. Place the dough in a greased bowl and cover it with a clean kitchen towel. Let it rise in a warm area for about 1 hour or until it has doubled in size.

5. Preheat your oven to 375°F (190°C). Grease a 8½ x 4½ x 2½-inch (21 x 11 x 6-cm) loaf pan and set it aside.

6. Once the dough has risen, punch it down to release any air bubbles. Transfer it to a floured surface and shape it into a loaf shape that fits your pan. Place the shaped dough into the greased loaf pan. If desired, you can brush the top of the dough with a little water and sprinkle some rolled oats on top.

7. Cover the loaf pan with the kitchen towel and let the dough rise for another 30 minutes.

8. Bake the bread in the preheated oven for 30 to 35 minutes or until the top is golden brown. Remove the loaf from the pan. Hold it with a towel in one hand and give it a few quick knocks with your knuckles to check doneness. If it's done, it will sound hollow. If not, return the loaf to the pan and bake in 5- to 10-minute increments.

9. Remove the bread from the oven and let it cool in the pan for about 10 minutes. Transfer it to a wire rack to cool completely before slicing.

Simple French Baguette

These long, crusty loaves are perfect for sandwiches, dipping in soup, or simply enjoyed on their own.

5½ cups (660 g) bread flour, plus more as needed

1 packet or 2¼ teaspoons (7 g) instant yeast

1 teaspoon (6 g) salt

2¼ cups (535 ml) water, warm (around 110°F [43°C])

1 tablespoon (15 ml) olive oil, plus more as needed

Makes 4 baguettes

1. In a large mixing bowl, combine the flour, yeast, and salt. Add the warm water and olive oil to the bowl and fold with a spatula until the ingredients are mostly combined. Sprinkle with a little more flour and knead until you form a ball. Do not overknead.

2. Lightly oil the glass bowl and place the dough ball in the bowl. Cover the bowl with plastic wrap and let it sit in a warm place to rise for 90 minutes. The dough should double in size.

3. Once the dough has doubled, punch it down and divide it into 4 equal pieces. Roll each piece of dough into a ball, cover with a clean towel, and let them rest for 15 to 20 minutes.

4. Flatten a piece of dough into a circle, fold the right side into the middle, and pinch together. Then, fold the right side once more all the way to the edge and pinch the ends and the seams together. Repeat the process with all the remaining pieces of dough.

5. Cover a large baking sheet with parchment paper and lightly flour it. Roll each piece of dough into a long, thin log, about 16 inches (41 cm). Place each log onto the prepared baking sheet. Let the dough logs rise for 1 hour until they have doubled in size. Ten minutes before the bread is finished rising, preheat the oven to 450°F (230°C).

6. Score the bread with a sharp knife or bread lame and bake for 20 minutes or until the bread is done and golden brown. You can baste it with vegan butter or olive oil.

TIPS:

For best results, use bread flour instead of organic unbleached all-purpose flour.

To achieve a crispy crust, add a shallow pan of water to the bottom of your oven while baking the baguette.

If you have a stand mixer with a dough hook attachment, you can use it to knead the dough instead of kneading by hand.

Pain de Campagne (Country Bread)

Boule is a classic type of bread that is perfect for any occasion. This loaf is characterized by its round shape and crusty exterior, with a soft and chewy interior. It is a perfect bread for sandwiches, toast, or as a side to any meal. Making a French boule from scratch might seem intimidating at first, but it is quite simple. With the right ingredients and a bit of patience, you can enjoy a delicious homemade boule in no time.

3 cups (375 g) organic unbleached all-purpose flour, plus more as needed

1¼ teaspoons (8 g) salt

¼ teaspoon (1 g) instant yeast

1½ cups (355 ml) water, warm (around 110°F [43°C])

Makes 1 round or oval loaf, 8 to 10 inches (20 to 25 cm) in diameter

1. Mix the flour, salt, and yeast in a large glass bowl. Stir in water to blend the ingredients. The dough should be shaggy, wet, and sticky. Cover the bowl with a clean towel and let it rest for 12 to 24 hours in a warm place.

2. When the surface is dotted with bubbles you are ready to move forward. Dump the dough onto a clean and generously floured work surface. Sprinkle the top with a little more flour and fold it a couple of times. Cover the dough with the towel and let it rest 15 more minutes.

3. Shape the dough into a ball and use just enough flour to keep your hands from sticking. Lay out a clean towel and coat it with flour. Lay the dough on it, seam-side down, and dust with flour. Use quite a bit to prevent the dough from sticking to the towel. Cover the dough with a towel and let it rise for 2 hours. The dough should double in size.

4. Thirty minutes before the dough is ready, preheat the oven to 450°F (230°C) and place a large cast iron Dutch oven, with the lid, inside of the oven to heat up.

5. When the dough is ready, remove the Dutch oven and drop the dough into it, seam-side up. It's going to look all messy, but no worries. Shake the pot so the bread can evenly settle. Cover the pot with the lid and bake for 30 minutes. Remove the lid and bake for another 15 to 30 minutes or until or until the top is browned.

6. Remove from the oven, take the bread out of the pot, and set it on a rack to cool. Slice, serve, and enjoy.

Cheap Whole Meal Peasant Sandwich Bread

This no-knead peasant bread is a delicious treat that combines simplicity, plant-based ingredients, and old-world charm. This loaf requires minimal effort and expertise, making it an ideal choice for busy individuals or those new to breadmaking. With its crusty exterior and soft, pillowy interior, Mama's no-knead bread is rustic, homey, and sure to please.

4 cups (500 g) bread flour

2 teaspoons (11 g) Morton's kosher salt

2 teaspoons (9 g) organic cane sugar

1 packet or 2¼ teaspoons (7 g) instant yeast

2 cups (475 ml) water, warm (around 110°F [43°C])

2 tablespoons (28 g) vegan butter, room temperature

Makes 2 round loaves, 10 inches (25 cm) in diameter

1. Whisk together the flour, salt, sugar, and instant yeast together in a large mixing bowl. Add the water and mix until the flour is fully absorbed and the ingredients evenly combined.

2. Cover the bowl with plastic wrap and set aside in a warm, draft-free place. Let it rise for at least an hour.

3. Preheat the oven to 425°F (220°C) and grease two large 1 quart (950 ml) oven-safe glass bowls with the vegan butter. Use a couple of forks to punch down the dough and scrape it from the sides of the bowl by pulling the dough toward the center as you scrape it down. Be sure to loosen the dough completely from all sides of the bowl. Take both forks, divide the dough into 2 equal halves, and set each half into the prepared bowls.

4. Sit the bowls near the oven and let the dough rise for 30 more minutes.

5. Put the bowls in the oven. Bake for 15 minutes, then reduce the heat to 375°F (190°C) and bake for 15 more minutes. Take the loaves out of the oven and dump the loaves onto cooling racks. The loaves should fall right out onto the cooling racks if the bowls were greased well. Let the bread cool for 10 minutes before slicing and enjoying.

Holy Challah Bread

Challah bread is a traditional Jewish bread that is usually made with eggs and honey. With just a few simple substitutions, it's easy to make a delicious vegan version of this bread. This is not the hardest bread to make, but it does require a little time, persistence, and braiding skill. Whether you're a vegan, have an egg allergy, or just want to try something new, this recipe is fun and rewarding—and it's a great special-occasion option when the moment calls for it.

1¼ cups (285 ml) water, room temperature

1 tablespoon (12 g) active dry yeast

⅓ cup (67 g) organic cane sugar

⅓ cup (80 ml) grapeseed oil, plus more as needed

5 cups (625 g) organic unbleached all-purpose flour, plus more as needed

1 tablespoon (16 g) Morton's kosher salt

Cooking spray

Unsweetened plant-based milk or maple syrup, optional

Makes two 14-inch (36-cm) braided loaves

1. Combine the room temperature water, active dry yeast, and sugar in a large bowl. Whisk until the yeast dissolves into the water, then let it sit for 3 minutes.

2. Into the same bowl, add the grapeseed oil and whisk until it's well combined. Add the organic unbleached all-purpose flour and salt to the bowl. Use a wooden spoon to incorporate the flour into the wet ingredients. Use your hands to pinch the dough until there are no dry streaks of flour left and the dough is shaggy. Cover the bowl with plastic wrap and let it sit for 10 minutes at room temperature.

3. Pour the dough out onto lightly floured work surface and knead it for 5 to 7 minutes until the dough is smooth and elastic. Don't use any extra flour if you don't have to; the dough will become less sticky as you knead.

4. Clean the bowl and coat it with 1 to 2 teaspoons of oil. Place the dough into the bowl and cover with plastic wrap. Let the dough rise at room temperature for 2 hours until the dough has doubled in size.

5. Dump the dough out onto a clean work surface and divide the dough into 2 equal pieces. Divide each half of dough into 3 pieces, and roll each piece out into a rope about 12 to 14 inches (30 to 36 cm) long. Pinch one end of the first half's ropes together and braid the ropes of dough together to make a loaf. Pinch the other ends together and tuck them under. Repeat with the second half of dough and place the loaves on a baking sheet lined with parchment paper.

6. Pull out a piece of plastic wrap large enough to cover the loaves, spray it with cooking spray, and lay it over the loaves with the oiled side down. Place the loaves in a warm, draft-free place and let them rise at room temperature for about 2 hours. Preheat your oven to 350°F (180°C).

7   To give the challahs a shiny crust, you can brush the top of the loaves with
    plant-based milk or maple syrup. Bake for 35 to 40 minutes, rotate 180 degrees
    halfway through baking, brush on more milk or maple syrup to add more shine
    to the bread if desired, and let the challah finish baking until the crust is a dark
    golden brown. Remove the loaves from the oven and let them cool completely
    before slicing.

Rustic Italian Bread

Italian cuisine is renowned for its delectable bread, and there's something undeniably special about this crusty, rustic Italian bread, which will impress even the most discerning bread connoisseurs. This is one amazing loaf!

3¼ cups organic unbleached flour (407 g) or bread flour (390 g), plus more as needed

1 teaspoon (6 g) sea salt

1 packet or 2¼ teaspoons (9 g) active dry yeast

1½ cups (355 ml) water, warm (around 110°F [43°C])

Cornmeal for the pizza stone

Makes 1 round loaf, 8 to 10 inches (20 to 25 cm) in diameter

1. Add the flour, salt, and yeast to a large glass mixing bowl and use a wooden spoon or spatula to mix everything until well combined.

2. Pour in the warm water and mix until everything combines to form a soft dough. The dough will be sticky, but that's totally fine and normal. Cover the bowl with a clean dish towel and let the dough rise for 2 to 3 hours at room temperature until it has doubled in size.

3. Sprinkle some flour on a clean surface and turn out the bread dough on it. Put some flour on your hands as you take the dough out of the bowl because it will be sticky. Don't freak out; that's normal and everything is fine.

4. Add more flour to your hands, fold the dough onto itself, and form it into a round ball. *Do not knead it!* In fact, don't mess with it any more than you absolutely must. Place the bread dough on top of a sheet of parchment paper and carve an X in the top of the loaf, or just make a few cuts across using a serrated knife or bread lame.

5. Move the racks in your oven to accommodate an ovenproof bowl on the bottom rack beneath the center rack. Place a baking stone on the center rack and preheat your oven to 450°F (230°C). Let the baking stone heat for 30 to 45 minutes. Place an ovenproof bowl with a few cups of water on the bottom rack. This will create steam and help the crust to become crispy while the bread bakes.

6. Sprinkle some flour or cornmeal on a piece of parchment paper, place the bread dough on top of the parchment paper, and set it aside while you preheat your oven. Carefully slide the bread dough from the parchment paper to the pizza stone. Bake 30 to 45 minutes until golden brown all over and the bread is cooked through.

7. Take the bread out of the oven, transfer it to a cooling rack, and allow it to completely cool before slicing.

Swiss Braided Bread (Zopf)

When it comes to Swiss culinary traditions, the *zopf* is a classic that stands out. With its beautifully braided appearance and buttery, soft texture, this rich bread has been enjoyed by generations. While traditional recipes call for eggs and butter, fear not: I am here to guide you through the process of making a mouthwatering vegan version.

1 cup (235 ml) + 2 tablespoons (28 ml) unsweetened plant-based milk, room temperature, divided

¼ cup (80 g) + 1 tablespoon (20 g) maple syrup or agave nectar, divided

1 packet or 2¼ teaspoons (7 g) instant yeast

4 cups (500 g) organic unbleached all-purpose flour, plus more as needed

1 teaspoon (6 g) salt

½ cup (112 g) vegan butter, melted, plus more as needed

Makes 1 braided loaf, 12 to 14 slices

1. In a small bowl, combine 1 cup (235 ml) plant-based milk and ¼ cup (80 g) maple syrup (or agave nectar); warm the mixture in the microwave for about 30 seconds, ensuring it's not too hot to the touch. Add the instant yeast and let it sit for 5 to 10 minutes until frothy.

2. In a large mixing bowl, combine the flour and salt. Create a well in the center and pour in the activated yeast mixture and melted vegan butter. Stir the ingredients together until a dough forms.

3. Transfer the dough onto a lightly floured surface and knead it for about 10 minutes until smooth and elastic. If the dough feels too sticky, gradually add more flour until it becomes manageable.

4. Place the kneaded dough in a greased bowl, cover it with a clean kitchen towel, and let it rise in a warm, draft-free area for about 1 to 1½ hours or until it has doubled in size.

5. After the dough has risen, punch it down to release the air. Divide it into 3 equal portions and roll each piece into a long strand about 20 to 24 inches (51 to 61 cm) in length. Join the 3 strands together at one end and begin braiding them, taking turns crossing the outer strands over the center one. Once you've reached the end, pinch the strands together and tuck them under for a neat finish.

6. Place the braided loaf on a baking sheet lined with parchment paper. Cover it with a kitchen towel and let it rise for another 30 to 45 minutes.

7. Preheat your oven to 375°F (190°C). In a small bowl, mix 2 tablespoons (28 ml) plant-based milk and 1 tablespoon (20 g) maple syrup or agave nectar for the glaze. Brush the glaze over the loaf gently.

8. Bake in the preheated oven for approximately 25 to 30 minutes, or until it turns golden brown. Remove the loaf from the sheet. Hold it with a towel in one hand and give it a few quick knocks with your knuckles to check doneness. If it's done, it will sound hollow. If not, return the loaf to the sheet and bake in 5- to 10-minute increments. Once baked, transfer to a wire rack and let it cool completely before slicing or tearing into it.

Swedish Knäckebröd Crispbread

Swedish crispbread, also known as *knäckebröd*, is a traditional bread that has gained popularity worldwide for its crunchy texture and versatile nature. Serve alongside your favorite plant-based spreads, hummus, or vegan cheeses. It also makes a fantastic base for open-faced sandwiches, allowing you to get creative with various toppings and flavors. Whether you're hosting a party or simply looking for a satisfying snack, these vegan crispbreads are sure to impress.

1½ cups (188 g) whole wheat flour

1 cup (125 g) organic unbleached all-purpose flour, plus more as needed

1 cup (128 g) rye flour

1 teaspoon (6 g) salt

1 teaspoon (4.6 g) baking powder

2 tablespoons (30 ml) olive oil

1 cup (235 ml) water, warm (around 110°F [43°C])

1 tablespoon (20 g) maple syrup, optional

Sesame seeds, flaxseeds, or other toppings of your choice

Makes 1 to 2 trays of crispbread, depending on the size cut

1. Start by preheating your oven to 425°F (220°C). Line a baking sheet with parchment paper.

2. In a large mixing bowl, combine the flours, salt, and baking powder. Stir until well combined.

3. Create a well in the center of the dry mixture and pour in the olive oil and warm water. If you prefer a slightly sweeter taste, add the optional maple syrup as well. Mix the ingredients together until a dough forms.

4. Transfer the dough to a lightly floured surface and knead it for a few minutes until it becomes smooth and elastic. If the dough is too sticky, you can add a little extra flour.

5. Divide the dough into smaller portions for easier handling (this is personal preference). Take one portion and roll it out as thinly as possible. The crispbread should be approximately ⅛ inch (3 mm) thick.

6. Sprinkle the rolled-out dough with sesame seeds, flaxseeds, or any other toppings of your choice. Press them gently into the dough to ensure they adhere.

7. Use a pizza cutter or a sharp knife to cut the dough into squares or rectangles. This will help the crispbread bake evenly and make it easier to break apart after baking.

8. Carefully transfer the cut pieces to the prepared baking sheet. Make sure to leave a little space between each piece to allow for even baking. Repeat with each dough portion.

9. Place the baking sheet in the preheated oven and bake for approximately 10 to 12 minutes or until the crispbread turns golden brown and crispy. Keep a close eye on them, as they can easily burn. Once baked, remove the crispbread from the oven and let them cool completely on a wire rack. They will become even crispier as they cool down. Store them in an airtight container to maintain their crunchiness.

No-Knead Dutch Oven Artisan Bread

I love this bread; it holds a very special place in my heart. This was one of the very first loaves of bread I ever made. It was a nearly effortless start on my path to discovering the delights of homemade breadmaking. There's something magical about the aroma of freshly baked bread wafting through the kitchen, filling our hearts with warmth and our taste buds with anticipation. While the thought of making bread from scratch might seem intimidating, fear not! With the no-knead Dutch oven bread technique, you can achieve artisanal loaves without the need for complex kneading or fancy equipment. Let's dive into the world of this effortless breadmaking method that will have you savoring homemade bakery delights in no time.

3 cups (375 g) organic unbleached all-purpose flour, plus more as needed

1½ teaspoons (9 g) salt

½ teaspoon (2 g) instant yeast

1½ cups (355 ml) water, warm (around 110°F [43°C])

Cornmeal for bottom of pan, optional

Makes 1 round loaf, 8 to 10 inches (20 to 25 cm) in diameter

1. In a large mixing bowl, combine the flour, salt, and yeast.

2. Add the lukewarm water and mix everything together with a wooden spoon or your hands until a shaggy dough forms. Avoid overmixing.

3. Cover the bowl with plastic wrap or a clean kitchen towel and let it rise at room temperature for 12 to 18 hours, or until the dough has doubled in size and is dotted with bubbles.

4. Preheat your oven to 450°F (230°C) and place the Dutch oven with its lid inside to preheat as well.

5. Carefully remove the preheated Dutch oven from the oven and sprinkle a little flour or cornmeal in the bottom of it to prevent sticking.

6. Gently transfer the risen dough to the Dutch oven, seam-side up. Place the lid back on and return the Dutch oven to the oven. Bake for 30 minutes.

7. Remove the lid and bake for an additional 10 to 15 minutes, or until the loaf is golden brown.

8. Once baked, carefully remove the bread from the Dutch oven and let it cool on a wire rack before slicing.

ADD IT!

Once you've mastered the basic no-knead Dutch oven bread recipe, the possibilities are endless. Feel free to experiment with different flours, such as whole wheat, rye, or spelt, to add unique flavors and textures. You can also incorporate various add-ins like herbs, vegan cheese, dried fruits, or nuts to create your signature loaves.

TIPS:

Don't be alarmed by the sticky, wet dough. It's supposed to be that way and will transform during the long fermentation period.

THE BEAUTY OF NO-KNEAD BREAD

No-knead bread is a game-changer for home bakers, as it eliminates the need for laborious kneading. This method was popularized by baker Jim Lahey, who introduced it in his cookbook *My Bread: The Revolutionary No-Work, No-Knead Method*. The secret lies in allowing the dough to ferment and develop gluten naturally over a longer period. With minimal effort, you can achieve a beautiful loaf with a crisp crust and a soft, airy crumb.

THE DUTCH OVEN ADVANTAGE

The Dutch oven is the unsung hero of this breadmaking technique. Its thick, heavy walls and tight-fitting lid create the perfect environment for baking bread. When preheated in the oven, the Dutch oven traps steam and creates a moist environment, which contributes to a professional-looking crust and a tender crumb. The enclosed space also mimics the conditions of a commercial bread oven, resulting in a loaf with excellent oven spring and a caramelized exterior.

Whole Wheat Artisan Bread

Get ready to embark on a journey to carb heaven with this Whole Wheat Artisan Bread recipe! This isn't your run-of-the-mill loaf—I'm talking about a rustic, hearty creation that'll have you buttering slices faster than you can say "carb-loading." So, roll up your sleeves, dust off that apron, and let's transport ourselves back to the days when bread wasn't just a food, but a symbol of civilization—albeit with a wholesome twist!

4 cups (500 g) whole wheat flour

2 teaspoons (12 g) salt

¾ teaspoon (3 g) active dry yeast

1 to 2 cups (235 to 475 ml) water, warm

Makes one 9-inch (23 cm) loaf

1. In a large mixing bowl, whisk together the flour, salt, and yeast.

2. Pour in the warm water and stir until the dough evenly comes together. It might be best to use your hands. Spray another large bowl with cooking spray, form the dough into a rough ball, and place it in the bottom of the greased bowl. Cover the bowl with plastic wrap and let it sit on the counter for 12 to 18 hours.

3. Preheat your oven to 475°F (230°C) and place a Dutch oven inside the oven to preheat as well. Once the oven is ready and the Dutch oven is hot, carefully remove the pot from the oven and take off the lid.

4. Spread a piece of parchment paper onto a clean surface. Flour your hands and gently remove the risen dough from the bowl and form it back into a rough ball. Place it on the parchment paper and drop it into your hot Dutch oven. Cover the Dutch oven with the lid and place it into the oven.

5. Bake for 30 minutes with the lid on and then remove the lid and let the bread bake another 15 minutes or until the crust is golden and crusty on the outside.

6. Carefully remove the Dutch oven from the oven and take the bread out. Allow it to cool on a wired rack.

7. Slice, serve, and enjoy!

Japanese Hokkaido Milk Bread

Indulge in the ethereal delight of Japanese milk bread, renowned for its unparalleled fluffy texture that effortlessly melts in the mouth. At the heart of this culinary marvel lies the technique of *tangzhong*, akin to crafting a roux. Through this method, a small portion of the bread's flour is mixed with liquid and heated, creating a paste that imbues the loaf with an irresistibly tender crumb. The result is a sublime harmony of taste and texture, making Japanese milk bread a true pleasure for the senses.

For *tangzhong*:

2 tablespoons (15 g) bread flour

¼ cup (60 ml) unsweetened plant-based milk

2 tablespoons (30 ml) water

For milk bread:

3 cups (360 g) bread flour, plus more as needed

¼ cup (50 g) organic cane sugar

1 packet or 2¼ teaspoons (7 g) instant yeast

½ teaspoon (3 g) sea salt

¾ cup (175 ml) unsweetened almond milk, warm (around 110°F [43°C])

To make the *tangzhong*:

1. Whisk together the bread flour, vegan milk, and water in a small saucepan until well combined. Place the pan on the stove over medium-high heat and stir for 1 to 2 minutes until the mixture thickens. It should look like pudding or a thick slurry. Remove the *tangzhong* from the heat, pour it into a small bowl, and allow it to cool in the fridge for 10 minutes. It's best to do this when you're assembling the rest of the ingredients.

To make the milk bread:

1. Add the bread flour, sugar, instant yeast, and sea salt to the bowl of a stand mixer and whisk all the ingredients together. Create a well in the center of the flour and slowly add the warm milk, vegan butter, and *tangzhong* mixture to the dry ingredients. Mix with a wooden spatula until everything is just incorporated. The dough should have a shaggy look.

2. Cover the bowl with a kitchen towel and let the dough rest for 15 minutes so the ingredients can meld together.

3. Using the dough hook of your stand mixer, knead the dough on medium speed for 15 minutes. Pause halfway through if you need to scrape down the sides of your bowl. If the dough seems to stick, add a couple of tablespoons of flour in the first 5 minutes of kneading. Pull the dough up and onto itself and shape into a smooth ball. Place on a floured surface.

4. Clean, dry, and lightly grease the mixing bowl; place the dough ball back into the bowl. Cover it with a clean dish towel and let it sit for at least 1 to 2 hours in a warm, draft-free space. The dough should double in size.

5. Punch down the dough with your fist, pull the sides in on each other, and fold the dough over a few times. Divide the dough into 4 equal balls and weigh them to make sure they are all identical. Pull and roll the dough ball pieces tight, cover them with a damp paper towel, and let them rest for about 15 to 20 minutes.

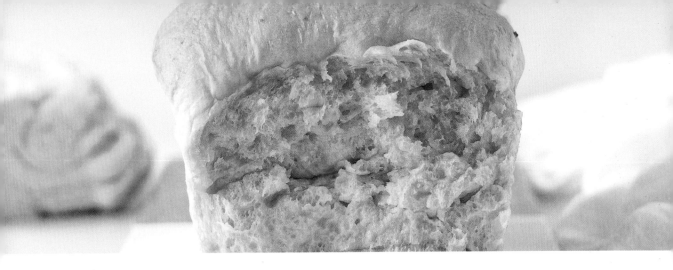

⅓ cup (75 g) vegan butter, melted, plus more as needed

3 tablespoons (45 ml) unsweetened plant-based milk

1 teaspoon (7 g) maple syrup

Makes one 8½ x 4½ x 2½-inch (21 x 11 x 6-cm) loaf

6. After 20 minutes, place one dough ball onto a lightly floured surface and use a rolling pin to gently roll the dough ball into a roughly 8 x 4-inch (20 x 10 cm) rectangle. Think flat and smooth. Fold the two ends over and onto each other. Turn the dough 90 degrees and roll it up. It should resemble a cinnamon roll about 4 inches (10 cm) wide.

7. Butter an 8½ x 4½ x 2½-inch (21 x 11 x 6-cm) loaf pan with vegan butter and place the first log into the loaf pan seam-side down. Repeat the process for the other 3 balls and place all the dough logs side by side in the loaf pan. Once again, cover with a damp towel and let it rise for about 45 minutes until the dough crowns over the top of the loaf pan. Within 15 minutes of the dough being finished, preheat your oven to 350°F (180°C) so it'll be ready to go when they're done rising.

8. Combine the unsweetened plant-based milk and maple syrup to make the vegan egg wash. Generously brush the dough logs with the mixture.

9. Bake the milk bread for 30 to 35 minutes on the middle oven rack. Remove from the oven. If the bread starts to brown too quickly, cover the loaf pan with foil for the last 10 minutes of baking.

10. Remove the bread from the oven, brush immediately with melted vegan butter, and let it sit for 10 minutes. Then, remove the bread from the pan and place it on a wire rack to cool. Enjoy your bread by pulling it apart or slicing it.

NOTE:

Wrap this bread and store it at room temperature for 5 to 7 days. If you prefer, you can freeze a loaf for up to 3 months. Let it thaw at room temperature before serving.

See page 114 for Loaded Sour Cream and Chive Bread recipe

Veggie, Nut, and Seed Breads

Seeded Share Bread

Herb and Seed Tear and Share Bread is a centerpiece perfect for gatherings. Placed in a bundt tin, they rise as the oven preheats. Amidst the joyful chaos of sharing, this Herb and Seed Tear and Share Bread isn't just nourishment for the body, it's a testament to the human art of creation, a celebration of gathering, and a reminder that in the world of food, as in life, there's truly something for everyone in the diversity of herbs and seeds.

2 cups (475 ml) water, lukewarm

1½ tablespoons (19 g) sugar

1 packet or 2¼ teaspoons (7 g) active dry yeast

1 teaspoon (6 g) salt

1 tablespoon (15 ml) olive oil

2 to 2½ cups (313 g) organic unbleached all-purpose flour

2 tablespoons (22 g) chia seed

2 tablespoons (8 g) fresh parsley, finely chopped

2 tablespoons (9 g) sesame seeds

2 tablespoons (9 g) sliced almonds

Makes one 9-inch (23-cm) loaf

1. In a large bowl, combine water, sugar, and yeast. Let it sit for 5 minutes until small bubbles appear on the surface.

2. Add olive oil, flour, and salt to the bowl. Mix until the dough forms. If it's too sticky, add a bit more flour. The dough should come together as one piece and not stick to your hands.

3. Knead the dough for 10 minutes. Then, place it in a bowl coated with oil and cover it with plastic wrap. Let it rise for about 60 minutes in a warm place, until it doubles in size.

4. After an hour, gently press out the air from the dough and shape it into small balls, like ping pong balls. Slightly wet the outside of each ball by dipping your fingers in water. Roll each ball in different toppings and place them into a non-stick Bundt tin.

5. Once all the dough balls are in the tin, cover it with plastic wrap and let them rise for another 30 minutes. Meanwhile, preheat your oven to 350°F (180°C).

6. Bake the bread for 30 to 35 minutes until it's golden brown. Let it cool in the tin for 20 minutes, then turn it out onto a wire rack to cool completely. It's best to enjoy the bread fresh on the same day it's made.

NOTE:

You can keep the bread in a sealed container for 2 to 3 days, but it's most delicious when enjoyed on the day of baking.

No-Knead Cheddar Onion Bread

There are no words, but I'll try. This cheddar and onion no-knead bread is freaking amazing! It's perfect for sandwiches, a side dish, or just on its own with a little vegan butter. It's packed with so much cheesy and savory flavor you'll have to convince yourself and those around that it's vegan.

3 cups (375 g) organic unbleached all-purpose flour

1 teaspoon (6 g) salt

¼ teaspoon (1 g) instant yeast

1 cup (120 g) finely chopped vegan cheddar cheese

¼ cup (25 g) finely chopped scallion

1½ cups (355 ml) water, warm (around 110°F [43°C])

Makes 1 round loaf, 8 to 10 inches (20 to 25 cm) in diameter

1. In a large mixing bowl, combine the flour, salt, and yeast. Mix well to combine.

2. Add the vegan cheddar cheese and scallion to the flour mixture. Mix well to combine.

3. Add the warm water to the bowl and mix well to form a shaggy dough. The dough will be sticky and wet.

4. Cover the bowl with a clean kitchen towel and let it sit at room temperature for 12 to 18 hours. During this time, the dough will rise and become bubbly.

5. Preheat your oven to 450°F (230°C). Place a large cast-iron pot with a lid in the oven while it preheats.

6. Remove the pot from the oven and carefully transfer the dough into the pot. Use a spatula to shape the dough if necessary.

7. Cover the pot with the lid and bake for 30 minutes. Remove the lid from the pot and bake for an additional 15 to 20 minutes, or until the bread is golden brown and crispy.

8. Remove the pot from the oven and let the bread cool for at least 10 minutes before slicing and serving.

Loaded Sour Cream and Chive Bread

If you're a fan of savory bread with a tangy twist, this sour cream and chive bread is perfect for you. It combines the creaminess of vegan sour cream with the aromatic freshness of chives, resulting in a delightful and moist loaf that will satisfy your taste buds.

2 cups organic unbleached all-purpose flour (250 g) or bread flour (240 g)

1 tablespoon (14 g) baking powder

1 teaspoon (6 g) salt

1 tablespoon (13 g) organic cane sugar

½ cup (115 g) vegan sour cream

½ cup (120 ml) unsweetened plant-based milk

2 tablespoons (6 g) + 1 tablespoon (3 g) finely chopped fresh chives, divided

1 tablespoon (14 g) vegan butter, melted

Sea salt flakes, optional

Makes one 9 x 5 x 3-inch (23 x 13 x 6-cm) loaf

1. Begin by preheating your oven to 375°F (190°C). Grease a 9 x 5 x 3-inch (23 x 13 x 6-cm) loaf pan and set it aside.

2. In a large mixing bowl, whisk together the flour, baking powder, salt, and sugar. Ensure the ingredients are well combined.

3. Create a well in the center of the dry ingredients and pour in the vegan sour cream and plant-based milk. Mix until just combined. Avoid overmixing, as it can result in a denser bread.

4. Gently fold in 2 tablespoons (6 g) finely chopped fresh chives, evenly distributing them throughout the batter.

5. Pour the batter into the greased loaf pan, spreading it evenly.

6. In a small bowl, combine the melted vegan butter and 1 tablespoon (3 g) finely chopped chives. Mix well.

7. Brush the butter and chive mixture evenly over the top of the bread batter. Sprinkle sea salt flakes on top for an extra burst of flavor, if desired.

8. Place the loaf pan in the preheated oven and bake for approximately 40 to 45 minutes, or until a toothpick inserted into the center comes out clean. The top should be golden brown.

9. Once baked, remove the bread from the oven and allow it to cool in the pan for about 10 minutes. Then, transfer it to a wire rack to cool completely before slicing. This will help the bread maintain its shape.

No-Knead Olive Bread

Introducing a culinary marvel that combines simplicity and sensational flavors—the Amazing No-Knead Olive Bread. This artisanal delight redefines homemade baking with its simple preparation method that requires no intricate kneading. Embark on a journey of delightful aromas and exquisite taste as the rich, briny notes of olives intertwine with perfectly textured bread, making every slice a delectable masterpiece.

3¼ cups (390 g) bread flour, plus more as needed

1 packet or 2¼ teaspoons (7 g) instant or active dry yeast

2 teaspoons (12 g) sea salt

2 teaspoons (2 g) Italian seasoning

1½ teaspoons (2.3 g) garlic powder

1 heaping cup (about 135 g) roughly chopped olives

1½ cups (355 ml) water, close to room temperature

Makes one 9-inch (23-cm) loaf

1. In a large mixing bowl, whisk the flour, yeast, salt, Italian seasoning, and garlic powder together. Using a wooden spoon, mix in the olives. Pour in the water and gently mix everything together. The dough will seem dry and shaggy but keep going until all the flour is moistened. If needed, use your hands to work the dough ingredients together. The dough will be sticky. Shape into a ball in the bowl as best you can.

2. Leave the dough in the bowl, cover the dough tightly with plastic wrap and let it rise for 2 to 3 hours at room temperature. The dough should almost double in size, stick to the sides of the bowl, and have a lot of air bubbles. Place the covered dough in the refrigerator for 12 hours and let it sit. It might deflate a bit but that's okay.

3. Lightly dust a large nonstick baking sheet with cornmeal or flour and turn the dough out onto a clean floured surface. Generously flour your hands and shape into a ball as best you can then transfer to prepared baking sheet. Cover with a clean towel and let the dough to rest for 45 minutes.

4. Preheat the oven to 425°F (218°C), while the dough is resting. When ready to bake, using a very sharp knife or bread lahm and score the dough with an X, about ½-inch (1-cm) deep. If your dough flattens out during this 45 minutes, flour your hands and reshape into a ball.

5. Place the dough in the oven on the center rack and bake for 35 to 40 minutes or until the crust is golden brown. Check for doneness by giving the warm loaf a light tap. If it sounds hollow, it's done. Remove the bread from the oven and let it cool for 20 minutes before slicing and serving. Loosely cover leftover and store at room temperature for 3 days.

Morning Muesli Bread

Muesli is packed with the goodness of oats, nuts, seeds, and dried fruits. It's one of those breads that is sure to keep you fueled and satisfied. Nourish your body with a homemade treat while the freshly baked aromas fill your kitchen.

1½ cups (355 ml) water, warm (around 110°F [43°C])

1 packet or 2¼ teaspoons (7 g) instant yeast

½ tablespoon (3 g) salt

3 cups (375 g) organic unbleached flour, plus more as needed

¼ cup (32 g) whole wheat flour

Cooking spray to grease bowl and baking sheet

¼ cup (35 g) raisins

1 cup (235 ml) water

¼ cup (30 g) chopped raw walnuts

¼ cup (28 g) chopped raw almonds

Makes 1 round or oval loaf, 8 to 10 inches (20 to 25 cm) in diameter

1. In a large mixing bowl, combine the water, yeast, salt, and flours; stir with a wooden spoon until well combined. It will yield a rough and sticky dough.

2. Lift the dough out, clean and dry the bowl, lightly grease the bowl with cooking spray, and place the dough back into the bowl. Cover the bowl with a clean kitchen towel and let the dough rise for 2 hours at room temperature and 2 hours in the fridge.

3. Thirty minutes before the bread is done rising, soak the raisins in a bowl of water, then drain, pat them dry, and set them aside. This will prevent the raisins from burning while the bread is baking.

4. Once the dough has risen, lightly sprinkle the dough with flour and turn out onto a clean floured work surface. Knead the dough for 20 to 30 seconds, then add the walnuts, almonds, and raisins. Knead once more until everything is just combined. Shape the dough into a loaf, making sure the nuts and raisins are inside the dough—you don't want them getting burned or too crispy.

5. Lightly grease a baking sheet, add the loaf, and lightly flour the top. Let it rest for 1 hour.

6. Preheat your oven to 450°F (230°C) while the dough is resting. Place a metal pan on the lowest oven rack to hold water for the steam bath.

7. When the oven is hot and you're ready to bake, use a serrated knife or bread lame to make 2 or 3 slashes on top of the loaf about ½-inch (1-cm) deep.

8. Place the bread in the oven, pour about 1 cup (235 ml) water into the metal pan on the bottom rack, and quickly close the oven door. Bake the bread for 25 to 35 minutes or until it turns a dark golden brown. Remove the bread from the oven and allow it to cool on a rack.

Tree Hugger Nut and Seed Bread

This vegan nut and seed bread is a delicious and nutritious option for those who follow a plant-based diet or simply enjoy a hearty homemade bread. Packed with an assortment of nuts and seeds, this bread is not only flavorful but also provides a good dose of healthy fats, fiber, and essential minerals. It is perfect as a hearty toast or for serving with dips like hummus.

1½ cups (120 g) rolled oats

½ cup (80 g) raw pumpkin seeds

½ cup (60 g) raw sunflower seeds

½ cup (50 g) raw walnuts, chopped

¼ cup (37 g) raw almonds, chopped

⅓ cup (48 g) sesame seeds

¼ cup (28 g) ground flaxseed

2 tablespoons (22 g) chia seeds

3 tablespoons (15 g) whole psyllium husks

1½ teaspoons (21 g) salt

2 tablespoons (40 g) maple syrup or agave nectar

3 tablespoons (45 ml) vegetable oil

1½ cups (355 ml) water

Makes one 8½ x 4½ x 2½-inch (21 x 11 x 6-cm) loaf

1. Combine the oats, pumpkin seeds, sunflower seeds, walnuts, almonds, sesame seeds, flaxseed, chia seeds, psyllium husks, and salt in a large mixing bowl and whisk until well combined.

2. Whisk the maple syrup or agave nectar, vegetable oil, and water together in a small mixing bowl.

3. Add the wet ingredients to the dry and mix with a wooden spoon or spatula until everything is completely soaked and well combined. If the dough is too thick to stir, add 1 to 2 tablespoons (15 to 28 ml) water.

4. Grease and line an 8½ x 4½ x 2½-inch (21 x 11 x 6-cm) loaf pan with parchment paper. Pour the mixture into the pan. Smooth out the top, cover with a clean towel, and let sit out on the counter for at least 3 to 4 hours.

5. Preheat oven to 375°F (190°C).

6. Place the loaf pan in the oven and bake for 20 minutes. After 20 minutes, remove bread from loaf pan and place it upside down directly on the oven rack. Bake another 30 to 40 minutes. Let bread cool completely before slicing.

NOTE:

Psyllium husks are usually sold in the natural section of grocery stores, in health food stores, or online.

Southern Sweet Potato Bread

Are you a banana bread fan? Just wait until you try this amazing vegan sweet potato bread! It has all the warming spices of fall but can be enjoyed year-round. It's easy to make and requires only a few simple ingredients. Whether you are a vegan or not, you will love the taste and texture of this sweet potato bread.

1 cup (110 g) chopped sweet potatoes

1 cup (200 g) organic cane sugar

½ cup (120 ml) vegetable oil

1 overripe banana

1¾ cups (219 g) organic unbleached all-purpose flour

1 teaspoon (5 g) baking soda

1 teaspoon (2 g) pumpkin pie spice

¼ teaspoon (2 g) salt

⅛ teaspoon (1 g) baking powder

⅓ cup (80 ml) water

¼ cup (30 g) chopped walnuts

Makes one 9 x 5 x 3–inch (23 x 13 x 6-cm) loaf

1. Place the sweet potatoes in a large pot, cover with water, and boil until tender and easily pierced with a fork, usually about 20 to 30 minutes. Drain the sweet potatoes and mash them with a fork or potato masher until they are smooth.

2. Preheat the oven to 350°F (180°C) and grease a 9 x 5 x 3-inch (23 x 13 x 6-cm) loaf pan.

3. In a large bowl, stir the sugar and oil together until well combined. Mash the peeled banana until smooth and then mix in with the sugar and oil.

4. Whisk together the flour, baking soda, pumpkin pie spice, salt, and baking powder in a separate bowl until well combined.

5. Stir the flour mixture into the wet mixture along with water until smooth. Fold in the sweet potatoes and walnuts, and stir until batter is smooth.

6. Pour the batter into the prepared loaf pan and bake for 1 hour or until the top is a dark golden brown.

7. Remove from the oven and let cool 5 minutes on a wire rack while still in the loaf pan. Then, remove from the loaf and let cool to room temperature. You can enjoy right away, but it's more dense once it has cooled.

Old-Fashioned Peanut Butter Bread

I stumbled upon a version of this recipe in an old cookbook from the 1940s that belonged to my great-grandmother. Peanut butter bread is a light, fluffy, and delicious quick bread that became popular during the Great Depression. A lot of families didn't have access to fresh ingredients during that time, but pantry ingredients like peanut butter, salt, flour, and baking powder were still readily available and inexpensive. Perfect for breakfast, dessert, or a snack.

2 cups (250 g) organic unbleached flour

2 teaspoons (9.2 g) baking powder

1 teaspoon (4.6 g) baking soda

¼ teaspoon (2 g) salt

1½ cups (355 ml) oat milk

½ cup (130 g) all-natural peanut butter

¼ cup (80 g) maple syrup

Makes one 8½ x 4½ x 2½-inch (21 x 11 x 6-cm) loaf

1. Preheat your oven to 350°F (180°C) and prepare a standard 8½ x 4½ x 2½-inch (21 x 11 x 6-cm) loaf pan by lining it with parchment paper.

2. Whisk the flour, baking powder, baking soda, and salt together in a large mixing bowl. In a separate bowl, mix the oat milk, peanut butter, and maple syrup together until it's smooth.

3. Add the wet ingredients to the dry ingredients and mix with a wooden spoon or spatula until well combined; be careful not to overmix the batter. Pour the batter into the prepared loaf pan and smooth out the top with a spatula.

4. Place the loaf pan on the middle rack of the oven and bake for 45 to 50 minutes, or until a toothpick inserted into the center of the bread comes out clean.

5. Let the bread cool in the pan for 5 to 10 minutes before transferring it to a wire rack to cool completely. Once the bread is completely cool, slice it and serve.

Plain and Simple Garlic Bread

Garlic bread is a timeless classic loved by many for its garlicky goodness and the irresistible combination of crispy exterior and soft, buttery interior. Use your French baguette to make delicious garlic bread!

½ cup (112 g) vegan butter, softened

4 cloves garlic, minced

2 tablespoons (8 g) fresh parsley, finely chopped

1 teaspoon (1 g) dried oregano

½ teaspoon (3 g) sea salt

1 large baguette or French bread

Vegan Parmesan cheese, for topping, optional

Makes at least 8 to 10 pieces, depending on the size of your bread

1. Preheat your oven to 375°F (190°C).

2. In a small bowl, combine the softened vegan butter, minced garlic, chopped parsley, dried oregano, and sea salt. Mix well until all the ingredients are evenly incorporated.

3. Slice the baguette or French bread lengthwise, creating two equal halves. Spread the garlic butter mixture generously on each cut side of the bread. Ensure that the mixture covers the entire surface for maximum flavor.

4. If desired, sprinkle some vegan Parmesan cheese on top of the garlic butter mixture for an extra layer of deliciousness. Place the bread halves on a baking sheet, cut-side up, and bake in the preheated oven for approximately 12 to 15 minutes or until the edges turn golden brown and crispy.

5. When the bread is baked, remove it from the oven and let it cool slightly. This step allows the garlic flavors to meld together and the butter to set a bit. Slice the garlic bread into smaller pieces, serve warm, and enjoy!

Morning Glory Sunflower Seed Bread

This delightful sunflower seed bread is packed with flavor, nutrients, and a satisfying crunch. With its nutty flavor, hearty texture, and abundance of plant-based goodness, this bread is a wonderful addition to any meal, but will help you rise and shine first thing in the morning.

1 tablespoon (7 g) ground flaxseed

3 tablespoons (45 ml) water

2 cups (250 g) organic unbleached all-purpose flour (or whole wheat flour for a heartier texture)

1 cup (145 g) raw sunflower seeds, plus extra for topping

2 teaspoons (9.2 g) baking powder

½ teaspoon (3 g) salt

1 cup (235 ml) unsweetened plant-based milk

2 tablespoons (40 g) maple syrup or agave nectar

Makes one 8½ x 4½ x 2½-inch (21 x 11 x 6-cm) loaf

1. Preheat your oven to 350°F (180°C) and line a 8½ x 4½ x 2½-inch (21 x 11 x 6-cm) loaf pan with parchment paper.

2. Prepare the flax egg. In a small bowl, mix the ground flaxseed with the water and set it aside for 5 minutes to thicken. This mixture will act as a binder in the absence of eggs.

3. In a large mixing bowl, combine the flour, sunflower seeds, baking powder, and salt. Stir well to ensure even distribution.

4. To the dry ingredients, add the plant-based milk, sweetener, and the prepared flax egg. Mix everything together with a wooden spoon until a thick, sticky batter forms. Make sure all the ingredients are fully incorporated, but be careful not to overmix.

5. Pour the batter into the prepared loaf pan, spreading it evenly with a spatula. Sprinkle additional sunflower seeds on top for added texture and visual appeal.

6. Place the loaf pan in the preheated oven and bake for approximately 45 to 50 minutes, or until the bread is golden brown and a toothpick inserted into the center comes out clean.

7. Once the bread is baked, remove it from the oven and allow it to cool in the pan for 10 minutes. Then, transfer it to a wire rack to cool completely. Once cooled, slice the bread into desired thickness.

TIPS AND VARIATIONS:

For an extra-nutty flavor, toast the sunflower seeds before adding them to the bread batter.

Feel free to customize your bread by adding herbs, spices, or even dried fruits for a touch of sweetness.

Experiment with different types of plant-based milk to find your preferred flavor profile.

Store the bread in an airtight container at room temperature for up to 3 to 4 days.

Alternatively, slice it and freeze it for longer shelf life.

*See page 139 for Orange
Cranberry Bread recipe*

CHAPTER
6

Fruit Breads and Sweet Loaves

Best Damn Vegan Banana Bread

With its moist texture, tropical aroma, and natural sweetness, this plant-based banana bread is sure to win the hearts of vegans and nonvegans alike. Feel free to experiment by adding nuts, vegan chocolate chips, or a hint of spice. Put on your apron, grab those ripe bananas, and embark on a delightful baking journey that's compassionate and irresistibly delicious!

3 overripe bananas

½ cup (161 g) maple syrup

⅓ cup (82 g) unsweetened apple sauce

1 teaspoon (5 ml) vanilla extract

1½ cups (250 g) whole wheat flour

¼ cup (28 g) ground flaxseed

1 teaspoon (4.6 g) baking soda

½ teaspoon (2.3 g) baking powder

½ teaspoon (1 g) ground cinnamon

¼ teaspoon (1.5 g) salt

Makes one 8½ x 4½ x 2½-inch (21 x 11 x 6-cm) loaf

1. Preheat your oven to 350°F (180°C) and line an 8½ x 4½ x 2½-inch (21 x 11 x 6-cm) loaf pan with parchment paper or use a nonstick loaf pan.

2. Place the peeled bananas in a large bowl and mash using a fork or potato masher. The bananas do not have to be completely smooth; it's ok to have some small chunks for texture. Add in the maple syrup, unsweetened apple sauce, and vanilla extract. Mix until everything is well combined.

3. To a separate bowl, add the flour, flaxseed, baking soda, baking powder, cinnamon, and salt; whisk them together. Add the dry mixture to the wet and mix until everything is just combined—*do not overmix.*

4. Pour the batter into the prepared loaf pan and bake for 45 to 50 minutes. The banana bread is done when you insert a knife or toothpick and it comes out clean. Keep in mind, all appliances are different, so cooking time can vary several minutes one way or the other.

5. Remove the banana bread from the oven and let it cool for a bit in the baking pan. Then, carefully remove it and allow it to cool on a cutting board or cooling rack, preferably to room temperature. The longer you let it set, the easier it will slice. The texture and flavor will get better as well.

Sunny Day Lemon Loaf

Get ready to zest up your life with this delightful lemon loaf! Packed with citrusy goodness and a whole lot of plant-based charm, this loaf will have you doing a happy dance in the kitchen—you'll be tempted to hide it from your friends and kids (don't worry, I won't tell!).

6 ounces (170 g) silken tofu

¼ cup (55 g) vegan butter, melted

1 cup (235 ml) + 1 tablespoon (15 ml) unsweetened plant-based milk, divided

1 cup (200 g) organic cane sugar

Zest from 1 lemon

2 tablespoons (30 ml) + 1 tablespoon (15 ml) fresh lemon juice

1 teaspoon (5 ml) vanilla extract

2 cups (250 g) organic unbleached all-purpose flour

½ teaspoon (3 g) salt

2 teaspoons (9 g) baking powder

¼ teaspoon (1 g) baking soda

1 cup (125 g) powdered sugar

Makes one 8½ x 4½ x 2½-inch (21 x 11 x 6-cm) loaf

1. Preheat oven to 350°F (180°C) and lightly grease an 8½ x 4½ x 2½-inch (21 x 11 x 6-cm) standard loaf pan or line it with parchment paper.

2. Add the tofu, butter, 1 cup (235 ml) nondairy milk, sugar, lemon zest, 2 tablespoons (30 ml) lemon juice, and vanilla extract to a blender and process until smooth.

3. In a large mixing bowl, whisk together the flour, salt, baking powder, and baking soda.

4. Pour the wet mixture into the dry and mix with a wooden spoon until everything is just combined. *Do not overmix.*

5. Pour into the prepared pan and bake for 35 to 45 minutes until golden brown and a toothpick inserted comes out clean. Let the loaf cool in the pan for 10 minutes, then move to a cooling rack.

6. While the loaf cools, begin preparing the icing by adding the powdered sugar, 1 tablespoon (15 ml) unsweetened plant-based milk, and 1 tablespoon (15 ml) lemon juice to a bowl and whisk until the mixture is smooth. When the loaf has cooled down, drizzle the glaze on top. Allow the glaze to harden before slicing and serving. Enjoy!

NOTE:

It is important to use freshly squeezed lemon juice for the best flavor.

Gooey Cinnamon Swirl Bread

This tender and moist bread is a mouthwatering combination of fluffy dough swirled with a heavenly mixture of cinnamon, sugar, and plant-based butter. Whether enjoyed as a breakfast delight or an afternoon snack, this vegan twist on a classic recipe will surely satisfy your cravings while aligning with your ethical and dietary choices.

¼ cup (60 ml) water, warm (around 110°F [43°C])

1 teaspoon (4 g) organic cane sugar

1 packet or 2¼ teaspoons (9 g) active dry yeast

½ cup (120 ml) soy milk

¼ cup (50 g) organic cane sugar

¼ cup (55 g) + ¼ cup (55 g) vegan butter, melted, divided, plus more as needed

¼ cup (57 g) overripe mashed banana

1 teaspoon (5 ml) vanilla extract

2½ to 3 cups (313 to 375 g) organic unbleached all-purpose flour, divided, plus more as needed

1 teaspoon (6 g) sea salt

1. In the bowl of a stand mixer fitted with the dough hook or in a large bowl (if mixing by hand), combine warm water, organic cane sugar, and yeast; let sit until foamy (about 5 minutes).

2. Add the soy milk, sugar, ¼ cup (55 g) melted butter, mashed banana, and vanilla extract; stir to combine.

3. Add 2 cups (250 g) flour, sea salt, and ½ teaspoon (1 g) cinnamon; stir until incorporated.

4. Add ¼ cup (31 g) flour at a time and combine until it forms a smooth but slightly tacky dough ball.

5. Form the dough into a ball and place it into a large, lightly oiled bowl. Cover with a damp kitchen towel and let it rise in a warm place for 1 hour or until it doubles in size.

6. While the dough is rising, make the cinnamon swirl. Combine 1 tablespoon (7 g) cinnamon with the light brown sugar and set it aside.

7. Line a 9 x 5 x 3-inch (23 x 13 x 6-cm) loaf pan with parchment paper and grease with vegan butter. Set aside.

8. Remove the dough from the bowl when it has doubled in size and place it on a well-floured surface. Roll the dough into an 18 x 9-inch (46 x 23-cm) rectangle about ¼ inch (6 mm) thick. Use the loaf pan to measure the 9-inch (23-cm) side; the dough needs to fit into the pan once it's rolled.

9. Brush ¼ cup (55 g) melted butter over the dough and then sprinkle the cinnamon sugar mixture on top of it.

10. Staring at one end of the rectangle, roll the dough tightly widthwise so the roll is 9 inches (23 cm) long, not 18 inches (46 cm) long. Place the dough in the prepared loaf pan seam-side down. Cover the pan with a damp kitchen towel and let it rise while you preheat the oven.

½ teaspoon (1 g) + 1 tablespoon (7 g) ground cinnamon, divided

¾ cup (170 g) packed light brown sugar

Makes one 9 x 5 x 3-inch (23 x 13 x 6-cm) loaf

11. Preheat the oven to 350°F (180°C).

12. Bake for 35 minutes or until the top is brown and the loaf sounds hollow when thumped. Check the bread after 20 minutes and cover with aluminum foil if the top is browning too quickly.

13. Remove the bread from the oven and let it cool in the pan for 20 to 30 minutes on a wire rack. Then, run a knife around the edges to release the bread from the pan, and place the cinnamon swirl loaf on a wire rack to cool completely before serving.

Island Coconut Pineapple Bread

This moist and luscious loaf is infused with sweet pineapple and creamy coconut, creating a tantalizing combination that will transport your taste buds to sun-soaked beaches. A tropical aroma fills the air as you savor the tender texture and succulent bursts of pineapple in each slice. Prepare to embark on a culinary journey with this perfect taste of the exotic.

2 cups (250 g) organic unbleached all-purpose flour, plus more as needed

1 teaspoon (5 g) baking powder

1 teaspoon (5 g) baking soda

½ teaspoon (3 g) salt

2 to 4 tablespoons (28 to 55 g) vegan butter, slightly softened

½ cup (100 g) organic cane sugar

1 tablespoon (7 g) ground flaxseed

3 tablespoons (45 ml) water

1 teaspoon (5 ml) vanilla extract

¼ cup (60 ml) soy milk

8-ounce (225 g) can crushed pineapple and juice

½ cup (68 g) chopped macadamia nuts

½ cup (43 g) shredded toasted coconut

Makes one 9 x 5 x 3-inch (23 x 13 x 6-cm) loaf

1. Preheat the oven to 350°F (180°C) and grease a 9 x 5 x 3-inch (23 x 13 x 6-cm) loaf pan.

2. Sift together the flour, baking powder, baking soda, and salt in large bowl.

3. In a separate large mixing bowl, whip the vegan butter and sugar until light and fluffy.

4. In a small bowl, combine the flaxseed and water. Let sit for a few minutes to combine into a flaxseed egg.

5. To the whipped sugar mixture, add the flour mixture, flaxseed egg, vanilla extract, soy milk, and crushed pineapple and juice. Stir with a wooden spoon or spatula until everything is just combined. Add a little more flour if needed. The dough should be sticky and not too thick. Fold in the macadamia nuts and coconut. Pour the batter into the prepared pan and bake for 1 hour.

6. Remove the loaf from the oven and let cool on a wire rack for 10 to 15 minutes. Slice, serve, and enjoy.

Perfect-Every-Time Vegan Zucchini Bread

Cinnamon and nutmeg are combined with healthy grated zucchini to make this incredible bread. It's oil-free, fluffy, moist, and delicious. Perfect for breakfast, dessert, a healthy snack, or just to use up some of the bounty of your summer garden.

1½ cups organic unbleached flour (188 g) or whole wheat pastry flour (144 g)

½ teaspoon (2.3 g) baking soda

½ teaspoon (2.3 g) baking powder

¼ teaspoon (1.5 g) salt

1 teaspoon (2 g) ground cinnamon

¼ teaspoon (.6 g) ground nutmeg

1 tablespoon (7 g) ground flaxseed

3 tablespoons (45 ml) water

¾ cup (185 g) unsweetened applesauce

½ cup (60 g) packed brown sugar

¼ cup (80 g) maple syrup

2 teaspoons (10 ml) vanilla extract

1 cup (120 g) grated zucchini (about 1 medium sized zucchini)

Makes one 8½ x 4½ x 2½-inch (21 x 11 x 6-cm) loaf

1. Preheat your oven to 350°F (180°C). Prepare an 8½ x 4½ x 2½-inch (21 x 11 x 6-cm) loaf pan: use a nonstick loaf pan, silicone loaf pan, or line a loaf pan with parchment paper.

2. In a large mixing bowl, whisk together the flour, baking soda, baking powder, salt, cinnamon, and nutmeg until everything is thoroughly combined.

3. Create a flax egg by mixing the flaxseed and water in a small bowl; let sit for a few minutes. In a separate mixing bowl, mix together the flax egg, applesauce, brown sugar, maple syrup, vanilla, and zucchini until everything is well combined. Pour the wet ingredients into the dry ingredients and gently mix until everything is just combined. *Do not overmix!*

4. Pour your batter into the prepared loaf pan and bake for 45 to 50 minutes. Baking time will depend on your appliance, so be sure to pay attention to your zucchini bread. The bread is done when you can insert a toothpick or knife into the center and it comes out mostly clean with no raw or runny batter.

5. Remove the zucchini bread from the oven and allow to cool in the pan for 10 to 15 minutes. Then, remove the bread from the loaf pan and let it sit on a wire rack until it has completely cooled. If you don't have a wire rack, just use a cutting board. Cover and store your leftovers for 3 to 4 days at room temperature.

Chocolate Chip Pumpkin Bread

This pumpkin bread is easy to make, perfectly moist, and completely oil-free. Made in one bowl with cozy autumn spices and dark chocolate chips, it's the only pumpkin bread recipe you'll ever need. This recipe is a testament to the fact that vegan desserts can be just as indulgent and flavorful as their nonvegan counterparts.

15-ounce (425 g) can pure pumpkin

½ cup (161 g) maple syrup

1 teaspoon (5 ml) vanilla extract

⅓ cup (82 g) unsweetened applesauce

¼ cup (28 g) ground flaxseed

1½ cups organic unbleached flour (188 g) or whole wheat pastry flour (144 g)

1 tablespoon (7 g) pumpkin pie spice

1 teaspoon (4.6 g) baking soda

½ teaspoon (2.3 g) baking powder

½ cup (88 g) vegan chocolate chips

Makes one 8½ x 4½ x 2½-inch (21 x 11 x 6-cm) loaf

1. Preheat the oven to 350°F (180°C). Prepare an 8½ x 4½ x 2½-inch (21 x 11 x 6-cm) loaf pan with parchment paper or cooking spray, or use a nonstick pan.

2. Mix pumpkin, maple syrup, vanilla, and unsweetened applesauce together in a large bowl.

3. Add the flaxseed, flour, pumpkin pie spice, baking soda, and baking powder to the pumpkin mixture and stir together until everything is well combined. Fold the chocolate chips into the batter.

4. Pour the mixture into the prepared loaf pan and bake for 40 to 50 minutes.

5. The loaf is done when a toothpick is inserted into the center and comes out clean, except for any melted chocolate chips.

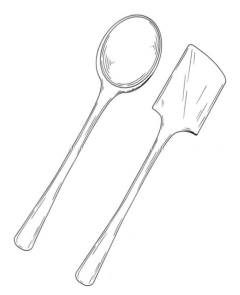

Apple Pie Bread

It's time to lose yourself in the comforting flavors of fall. Imagine the warm scent of cinnamon and nutmeg filling your kitchen as you bite into tender chunks of juicy apples nestled within a perfectly spiced batter. Get ready to savor the cozy flavors of autumn with our vegan apple pie bread—a slice of seasonal bliss.

2 apples, peeled, cored, and chopped

1 tablespoon (15 ml) + 1 tablespoon (15 ml) +1 tablespoon (15 ml) lemon juice, divided

¾ cup (175 ml) soy milk

2 cups (250 g) organic unbleached all-purpose flour

2 teaspoons (9 g) baking powder

1 teaspoon (5 g) baking soda

½ teaspoon (3 g) salt

½ teaspoon (1 g) + ½ teaspoon (1 g) ground cinnamon, divided

¼ cup (28 g) vegan butter, slightly softened

½ cup (100 g) organic cane sugar

½ cup (125 g) unsweetened apple-sauce

¼ cup (57 g) overripe mashed banana

1 teaspoon (5 ml) vanilla extract

½ cup (115 g) packed brown sugar

½ cup (63 g) powdered sugar

Makes one 9 x 5 x 3-inch (23 x 13 x 6-cm) loaf

1. Preheat your oven to 350°F (180°C) and line a 9 x 5 x 3-inch (23 x 13 x 6-cm) loaf pan with parchment paper.

2. In a small bowl, toss the chopped apples with 1 tablespoon (15 ml) lemon juice.

3. Whisk together 1 tablespoon (15 ml) lemon juice and soy milk in a small bowl. Set aside for 10 minutes.

4. Mix the flour, baking powder, baking soda, salt, and ½ teaspoon (1 g) cinnamon in a separate bowl.

5. In a large bowl, add the vegan butter and sugar and beat until light and creamy. Add the apple sauce and soymilk mixture and beat together. It will look a bit curdled, but that's totally fine. Add the cane sugar, banana, and vanilla extract and mix until everything is just blended.

6. Add the brown sugar and ½ teaspoon (1 g) cinnamon to the bowl of apples and toss to coat evenly.

7. In the prepared loaf pan, add half of the batter and top with half of the apple mixture. Use your hands or a wooden spoon to push batter and apple mixture into the corners. Top with the remaining batter and the rest of the apple mixture. Place the loaf pan in the oven and bake for 50 to 55 minutes or until a toothpick or knife comes out clean when inserted into the center of the loaf.

8. Mix together 1 tablespoon (15 ml) lemon juice and the powdered sugar to create the glaze. When the loaf is mostly cool, drizzle with glaze.

Orange Cranberry Bread

This moist and tender loaf is a delightful fusion of tart cranberries, orange zest, warming fall spices, and a perfect balance of sweetness. With its vibrant flavors and eye-catching crimson hues, this recipe is a delightful addition to any brunch table or afternoon tea. Each bite is a burst of juicy cranberries and citrus, guaranteed to have you craving more.

2 cups organic unbleached all-purpose flour (250 g) or whole wheat pastry flour (192 g)

⅔ cup (133 g) organic cane sugar

2 teaspoons (9 g) baking powder

½ teaspoon (2 g) baking soda

¼ teaspoon (1.5 g) salt

½ cup (125 g) unsweetened applesauce

1 cup (235 ml) orange juice

1 teaspoon (5 ml) vanilla extract

1 cup (100 g) fresh or frozen cranberries, plus more for topping

1 tablespoon (6 g) orange zest

Makes one 9 x 5 x 3–inch (23 x 13 x 6–cm) loaf

1. Put an oven rack in the center of the oven and preheat your oven to 350°F (180°C) and lightly grease a 9 x 5 x 3-inch (23 x 13 x 6-cm) loaf pan.

2. In a mixing bowl, add the flour, sugar, baking powder, baking soda, and salt; stir to combine.

3. Add in the applesauce, orange juice, and vanilla and mix until the dry ingredients are incorporated; don't overmix. Fold in 1 cup (100 g) cranberries along with the orange zest. Stir a couple of times, making sure everything is incorporated evenly.

4. Pour the batter into the prepared loaf pan, drop a few more cranberries on top, and bake on the center rack in the oven for 50 to 55 minutes.

5. Remove from oven and let cool before slicing. Store in an airtight container on the counter for up to 3 days or in the refrigerator for up to 7 days. The loaf will store in a freezer for up to 2 months; let thaw in the refrigerator before enjoying.

See photo page 126 for this recipe

See page 152 for Two-Ingredient Lentil Flatbread recipe

Flatbreads

Easy Peasy Whole Wheat Pita

Pita bread, a staple in Middle Eastern and Mediterranean cuisines, is a versatile and delicious bread. While traditional pita bread is made with refined white flour, why not have a healthier alternative? With just a few basic ingredients and a little patience, you'll be able to enjoy the aroma and taste of freshly baked, wholesome pita bread right from your own kitchen. Enjoy it with hummus, falafel sandwiches, or fill it up with whatever you choose.

1¼ cups (285 ml) water, warm (around 110°F [43°C])

1 tablespoon (20 g) honey or maple syrup

1 tablespoon (15 ml) olive oil, plus more as needed

1 packet or 2¼ teaspoons (9 g) active dry yeast

2 cups (250 g) whole wheat flour

1 cup (125 g) organic unbleached all-purpose flour, plus more as needed

1½ teaspoons (9 g) salt

Makes 8 pitas

1. In a small bowl, combine the warm water, honey or maple syrup, olive oil, and yeast. Stir gently and let it sit for about 5 to 10 minutes until it becomes frothy. This indicates that the yeast is active.

2. In a large mixing bowl, combine the flours and salt. Make a well in the center and pour in the yeast mixture. Gradually incorporate the dry ingredients into the wet mixture, stirring with a spoon or your hands until a shaggy dough forms.

3. Transfer the dough onto a lightly floured surface and knead for about 8 to 10 minutes until it becomes smooth and elastic. If the dough feels too sticky, add a little more flour, but be cautious not to add too much, as it may make the pita bread dense.

4. Grease a clean bowl with olive oil and place the kneaded dough in it. Cover the bowl with a damp cloth or plastic wrap and let it rise in a warm, draft-free area for about 1 to 2 hours until it doubles in size.

5. While the dough is rising, preheat your oven to 475°F (240°C) and place a baking stone or a large baking sheet inside to heat up.

6. Once the dough has risen, gently punch it down to release any air bubbles. Transfer it to a floured surface and divide it into 8 equal portions. Shape each portion into a smooth ball and let them rest for about 10 minutes to relax the gluten.

7. Take one ball of dough and roll it out into a circle approximately 6 to 7 inches (15 to 18 cm) in diameter. If the dough starts to shrink back, let it rest for a few more minutes and then continue rolling.

8. Carefully place the rolled-out dough onto the preheated baking stone or baking sheet. Depending on the size of your oven, you may be able to bake multiple pitas at once. Bake for about 3 to 4 minutes, or until the pita bread puffs up and starts to develop light golden-brown spots.

9. Continue rolling out and baking the remaining dough balls until all the pita bread is cooked. As each pita bread comes out of the oven, transfer it to a clean kitchen towel and cover it to keep it soft and pliable.

Garlic Herb Vegan Naan Bread

If you're a fan of Indian cuisine, you've likely enjoyed the deliciously soft and pillowy naan bread that often accompanies your meal. And while traditional naan is made with milk or yogurt, there's no reason why you can't make a plant-based version that's just as tasty. Note that more yeast than usual is called for to create air pockets.

½ cup (120 ml) water, warm (around 110°F [43°C])

1 tablespoon (13 g) organic cane sugar

1 tablespoon (12 g) active dry yeast

2 cups (250 g) organic unbleached all-purpose flour, plus more as needed

½ teaspoon (2 g) baking powder

½ teaspoon (3 g) salt

¼ cup (59 ml) vegetable oil

2 cloves garlic, minced

2 tablespoon (8 g) chopped fresh herbs, such as cilantro or parsley

Makes 6 to 8 naan

1. In a small bowl, combine warm water, sugar, and yeast. Mix well and let it sit for about 5 to 10 minutes, or until it becomes frothy.

2. In a large mixing bowl, combine flour, baking powder, and salt. Mix well. Add the frothy yeast mixture and vegetable oil to the flour mixture. Mix until a dough forms.

3. Knead the dough on a floured surface for about 5 to 10 minutes, or until it becomes smooth and elastic.

4. Place the dough in a greased bowl, cover it with a cloth, and let it rise in a warm place for about an hour, or until it doubles in size.

5. Preheat a skillet or a griddle over medium-high heat.

6. Divide the dough into 6 to 8 equal portions and roll each one into a ball. Flatten each ball and shape it into an oval.

7. In a small bowl, mix together the minced garlic and chopped herbs. Spread the garlic and herb mixture over the top of each naan.

8. Place the naan on the preheated skillet or griddle and cook for about 1 to 2 minutes, or until bubbles start to form. Flip the naan and cook for another 1 to 2 minutes, or until slightly browned and cooked through. Repeat with all of the dough.

Two-Ingredient Corn Tortillas

Corn tortillas are a staple of Mexican cuisine and a versatile foundation for countless dishes. Making your own from scratch is a wonderful way to save money, bring the flavors and traditions of Mexico into your kitchen, and know what you're eating is pure and unprocessed. With just a few simple ingredients and a tortilla press, you can create delicious, fresh tortillas. Not only will you enjoy the freshest and most authentic taste, but the process itself can be a fun and rewarding culinary adventure.

2 cups (186 g) masa harina, plus more as needed (corn flour specifically for tortillas)

1¼ cups (285 ml) water, room temperature, plus more as needed

½ teaspoon (3 g) salt (optional)

Makes about 12 corn tortillas

1. In a large mixing bowl, combine the masa harina and salt (if using). Gradually add the warm water to the bowl while stirring with a wooden spoon or your hands. Continue mixing until the dough comes together and forms a soft, pliable ball. It should be slightly sticky but not wet. If the dough feels too dry, add a little more water; if too wet, sprinkle in more masa harina.

2. Once the dough is well mixed, cover the bowl with a clean kitchen towel or plastic wrap.

3. Let the dough rest for at least 15 minutes, allowing the masa to fully hydrate and become more manageable.

4. After the resting period, divide the dough into approximately 12 equal-sized balls. However, the size of the balls will determine the desired tortilla size; if you want smaller tortillas, make smaller balls. Cover the balls again with the kitchen towel to prevent them from drying out.

5. Prepare your tortilla press by lining it with two pieces of plastic wrap or cut plastic bags. Take one masa ball and place it in the center of the tortilla press. Gently press the top of the press down, applying even pressure until the ball flattens into a thin, round tortilla. Carefully remove the tortilla from the press and set it aside. Repeat the process with the remaining balls.

6. Heat a dry nonstick skillet or griddle over medium-high heat. Once the skillet is hot, place a tortilla on the surface and cook for about 30 seconds to 1 minute per side, or until light golden-brown spots start to appear. Flip the tortilla and repeat the process. Remove the cooked tortilla from the skillet and place it in a tortilla warmer or wrap in a clean kitchen towel to keep it warm and pliable. Repeat the cooking process with the remaining tortillas, stacking them as you go.

7. Enjoy your versatile, freshly made corn tortillas in a variety of dishes. Use them to create tacos, enchiladas, quesadillas, and more. Don't forget to serve your tortillas with traditional Mexican accompaniments like salsa, guacamole, or pico de gallo for an authentic flavor experience.

Pizza Party Pull-Apart Bread

Vegan pizza pull-apart bread is a fantastic way to enjoy the flavors of pizza while also sharing a delicious and interactive treat. It has a flavorful dough, melty vegan cheese, and aromatic toppings!

For dough:

¾ cup (175 ml) water, warm

1 packet or 2¼ teaspoons (9 g) active dry yeast

1 teaspoon (4 g) organic cane sugar

2 tablespoons (30 ml) olive oil

1 teaspoon (6 g) salt

2 cups (250 g) organic unbleached all-purpose flour, plus more as needed

Cooking spray

For cheese:

½ cup (68 g) raw cashews

1 cup (235 ml) water

1 tablespoon (15 ml) lemon juice

1 teaspoon (5 ml) apple cider vinegar

1½ teaspoons (5 g) nutritional yeast

1 teaspoon (3 g) garlic powder

¼ cup (29 g) tapioca flour

½ teaspoon (3 g) salt

For serving:

2 tablespoons (28 g) vegan butter, melted

1 tablespoon (3 g) Italian seasoning

Marinara sauce

Makes 12 to 14 pieces

1. Stir the warm water, yeast, and sugar together and let activate for 10 minutes until foamy. Stir in oil and salt. Mix in ½ cup (63 g) flour at a time.

2. Knead the dough using your hands or a dough hook in a stand mixer until it forms a sticky ball. If it's too sticky, add 2 tablespoons (8 g) flour at a time until it comes together. Knead for 5 minutes.

3. Spray a glass bowl with cooking spray and place the dough ball into it. Cover the bowl with a towel and let it rise for 1 hour or until it doubles in size.

4. Punch the dough down and knead a couple of times until it becomes smooth and firm. Form the dough into a ball, wrap it in plastic wrap, and store the dough in the freezer or fridge until later.

5. For the cheese, add the cashews, hot water, lemon juice, vinegar, nutritional yeast, garlic powder, tapioca flour, and salt to a blender and blend until the mixture is completely smooth. Pour the mixture into a nonstick skillet; constantly stir over medium heat until the mixture starts to thicken and looks like melty mozzarella.

6. Preheat your oven to 425°F (220°C) and line a baking sheet with parchment paper.

7. Cut the dough into 12 to 14 equal pieces, add some vegan cheese to the middle of each piece, and roll together into a ball. Place the balls on the baking sheet with a little space between them. Add more vegan cheese in the spaces between the balls.

8. Combine the butter and Italian seasoning in a bowl. Brush the rolls and bake for 20 to 25 minutes until golden brown. Serve hot with marinara!

Rosemary Sesame Crackers

These homemade crackers are crispy, flavorful, and perfect for any occasion. Infused with the earthy essence of rosemary and the nutty allure of sesame seeds, they offer a delightful and delicate balance of flavors and textures. Their fragrant aroma and satisfying crunch will keep you coming back for more. Let's dive into the recipe and create a batch of these irresistible crackers!

1 cup (125 g) organic unbleached all-purpose flour

¼ cup (36 g) sesame seeds

1 tablespoon (3 g) dried rosemary, crushed

½ teaspoon (3 g) salt

¼ teaspoon (0.5 g) ground black pepper

3 tablespoons (45 ml) olive oil

¼ cup (60 ml) water

Makes 30 to 35 crackers

1. Preheat your oven to 350°F (180°C) and line a baking sheet with parchment paper.

2. In a large bowl, combine the organic unbleached all-purpose flour, sesame seeds, crushed dried rosemary, salt, and black pepper. Mix well to evenly distribute the ingredients.

3. Add the olive oil to the dry mixture and stir until the mixture becomes crumbly. Slowly pour in the water, a little at a time, and mix until a firm dough forms. You may not need all of the water, so add it gradually. Transfer the dough onto a lightly floured surface and knead it gently for a minute or two until it becomes smooth and elastic.

4. Divide the dough into 2 equal portions. Take 1 portion and roll it out into a thin rectangle or square shape about ⅛ inch (3 mm) thick. Repeat the same with the second portion. Using a pizza cutter or a sharp knife, cut the rolled-out dough into small cracker-sized squares or rectangles. Alternatively, you can use cookie cutters to create different shapes.

5. Carefully transfer the cut crackers onto the prepared baking sheet, leaving a little space between each cracker. Bake the crackers in the preheated oven for 12 to 15 minutes, or until they turn golden brown and crispy. Keep a close eye on them, as baking times may vary.

6. Once baked, remove the crackers from the oven and allow them to cool on a wire rack. They will become crispier as they cool down. Repeat the baking process with any remaining dough.

7. Once the crackers have completely cooled, store them in an airtight container to maintain their crispness. They can be enjoyed immediately or kept for several days.

Crunchy Breadsticks

These golden-brown delights are the perfect combination of light and airy with a satisfyingly crispy exterior. Whether enjoyed as a stand-alone snack, paired with a warm bowl of soup, or dipped in your favorite marinara sauce, these crunchy delights are sure to please your taste buds and leave you reaching for seconds.

¼ cup (60 ml) water, warm (around 110°F [43°C])

1 teaspoon (14 g) vegan butter

½ teaspoon (2 g) active dry yeast

1 cup (120 g) bread flour, plus more as needed

1 tablespoon (15 ml) olive oil

½ teaspoon (3 g) salt

¼ cup (55 g) vegan butter, melted

1 teaspoon (3 g) black sesame seeds, optional

½ teaspoon (3 g) coarse sea salt, optional

Makes 12 breadsticks

1. Add the warm water, butter, and yeast to a large mixing bowl; mix using a wooden spoon until both the yeast and butter have dissolved.

2. Add in the flour, oil, and salt and mix to form a dough. Knead on a lightly floured surface for around 5 minutes until the dough is smooth.

3. Place the dough back in the bowl, cover with plastic wrap, and set in a warm spot to rise for an hour.

4. Preheat the oven to 375°F (190°C), line a baking tray with parchment paper, and set aside.

5. Divide the dough into 12 pieces and roll each piece into a log about ½ inch (1 cm) thin. Place the breadstick on the prepared baking tray. If you like, brush them with a little melted vegan butter and sprinkle with black sesame seeds and coarse sea salt.

6. Bake in the middle of the oven for around 20 minutes or until golden. Store in an airtight container.

Two-Ingredient Oat Flatbread

In the world of baking, sometimes the most satisfying creations are the simplest ones. If you're looking for a quick and easy recipe that requires minimal ingredients and effort, then you're in for a treat. This recipe, made with just oats and water, creates a versatile and healthy flatbread that can be enjoyed in countless ways. The texture is like a thick, chewy burrito.

1 cup (80 g) rolled oats

1¼ cups (285 ml) water, boiling

Pinch salt, optional

Makes 6 to 7 flatbreads

1. Preheat a nonstick skillet over medium heat.

2. Add the oats, hot water, and a pinch of salt, if desired, to a blender. Blend until smooth.

3. Pour ⅓ cup (80 ml) batter into the pan and let cook for 2 to 3 minutes until you start to see dry spots. Flip and cook for 1 to 2 more minutes.

4. Repeat until you've used all the batter.

Two-Ingredient Lentil Flatbread

When it comes to quick and easy recipes, few can match the simplicity and deliciousness of a two-ingredient dish. So, the next time you're craving a warm, homemade bread without the fuss, give this two-ingredient red lentil flatbread a try. Prepare yourself for a delightful culinary experience that is not only simple but also packed with protein and fiber.

1 cup (192 g) dry red lentils

1¾ cups (425 ml) water

Makes 6 to 7 flatbreads

1. Place the red lentils in a high-speed blender and blend until they resemble a fine flour. Work in batches if needed.

2. Transfer to a bowl, add the water, and combine with a whisk. Let the batter sit for 2 to 3 minutes so the lentils absorb some of the water and the mixture becomes thicker.

3. Heat a nonstick frying pan over medium heat. Pour in ⅓ cup (80 ml) batter. Cook 2 to 3 minutes over medium heat, then flip over and cook 1 to 2 minutes on the other side. Remove to a covered plate to keep warm. Repeat until all batter is used.

ADD IT!
When the batter is complete, you can add in ¼ cup of raisins (35 g), chopped walnuts (30 g), nondairy dark chocolate chips or chunks (44 g), or diced pears (40 g).

ACKNOWLEDGMENTS

First of all, thank you to all the vegan bakers who devote themselves day in and day out to creating true culinary masterpieces—you are the true artisans. I by no means consider myself a master baker, by any stretch, but I took everything I could learn from you, my heroes, and tried to create the best recipes I could. THANK YOU so much to the ones who knead, twist, bake, and share your compassionate gift with me and the rest of the world.

Now, specific thank-yous:

Dan Rosenberg: This book and opportunity would have never happened without you. Thank you for taking a chance on someone who had never written a book and guiding me with your experience and wisdom.

Kerri Landis: Your patience and precise copy editing are truly awe-inspiring (I am attention-to-detail-challenged). Every email of corrections was always accompanied with kindness and encouragement. Thank you!

Anne Re: I still can't believe you let me be the photographer on this project. And, I'm sure I caused you to pull your hair out a time or two for taking so long. Your vision and creativity is something I could only aspire to.

Eric and Stephanie Hunt: Your friendship is indescribable. Thank you so much for the way you have loved me and my family all these years and encouraged me in my crazy pursuit of blogging. There are no words that even begin to describe how much my family and I love you.

Tim and Melissa Gremore: Thank you for being a soft and safe place to land in some hard times.

David and Julie Suter: Here's to 80s music and Cards Against Humanity. I love you both so much.

Fred and Katy Murchison: It's time for another Beech Mountain retreat. Andrea and I love you both very much!

Brett and Diane Kiser: You're the best in-laws in the universe.

Stephen Medlin: Thank you for always being a constant source of encouragement and accountability. Love you, brother!

Tom Ryan: Your comments and encouraging story kept me going early on in my blog journey. Thank you for making yourself available and offering me valuable insight when I first started on this journey of writing a book.

My children, Maddie, Jonathan, Macy, Mackenzie, and Millie-Jane: Y'all are my greatest creations and most valuable treasures. I love you!

Finally, and most importantly, thank you to my wife, Andrea! You took a job almost 25 years ago you would never have applied for: my wife. Your unconditional love and unwavering support for me is beyond what I deserve and can't imagine life with you.

About the Author

S hane Martin is the creator of the popular plant-based food blog, Shane & Simple, which is dedicated to creating delicious recipes centered around a whole food, plant-based diet. Shane is a culinary enthusiast who has transformed countless lives through his passion for plant-based eating. A true advocate for healthy living and sustainability, Shane's journey toward a plant-based diet has been nothing short of inspiring. Through his blog, he shares his profound knowledge of flavorful and nutritious plant-based recipes, making them accessible to everyone seeking a healthier lifestyle. Shane's vibrant personality and unwavering commitment to promoting a compassionate and environmentally friendly approach to food have earned him a devoted following and established him as one of the top vegan food blogs of the plant-based food movement.

INDEX